My previous editor is getting married. I'm as happy as if it were happening to me!

—Tite Kubo

BLEACH is author Tite Kubo's second title. Kubo made his debut with ZOMBIEPOWDER., a four-volume series for WEEKLY SHONEN JUMP. To date, BLEACH has been translated into numerous languages and has also inspired an animated TV series that began airing in the U.S. in 2006. Beginning its serialization in 2001, BLEACH is still a mainstay in the pages of WEEKLY SHONEN JUMP. In 2005, BLEACH was awarded the prestigious Shogakukan Manga Award in the *shonen* (boys) category.

BLEACH
VOL. 61: THE LAST 9 DAYS
SHONEN JUMP Manga Edition

STORY AND ART BY
TITE KUBO

Translation/Joe Yamazaki
Touch-up Art & Lettering/Mark McMurray
Design/Kam Li
Editor/Alexis Kirsch

BLEACH © 2001 by Tite Kubo. All rights reserved. First published in Japan in 2001 by SHUEISHA Inc., Tokyo. English translation rights arranged by SHUEISHA Inc.

The stories, characters and incidents mentioned in this publication are entirely fictional.

No portion of this book may be reproduced or transmitted in any form or by any means without written permission from the copyright holders.

Printed in the U.S.A.

Published by VIZ Media, LLC
P.O. Box 77010
San Francisco, CA 94107

10 9 8 7 6 5 4 3 2 1
First printing, August 2014

PARENTAL ADVISORY
BLEACH is rated T for Teen and is recommended for ages 13 and up. This volume contains fantasy violence.
ratings.viz.com

I believe the world is full of danger
I want to protect you from it
Only because inside me is the same impulse as that danger

BLEACH 61 THE LAST 9 DAYS

Shonen Jump Manga

ALL STARS AND

京楽春水
キョウラクシュンスイ
SHUNSUI KYORAKU

ZANGETSU
斬月
ザンゲツ

黒崎一護
クロサキイチゴ
ICHIGO KUROSAKI

plot

Ichigo Kurosaki meets Soul Reaper Rukia Kuchiki and ends up helping her eradicate Hollows. After developing his powers as a Soul Reaper, Ichigo enters battle against Aizen and his dark ambitions! Ichigo finally defeats Aizen in exchange for his powers as a Soul Reaper.

With the battle over, Ichigo regains his normal life. But his tranquil days end when he meets Ginjo, who offers to help Ichigo get his powers back. But it was all a plot by Ginjo to steal Ichigo's new powers! Ginjo, who was the first ever Deputy Soul Reaper, then reveals to Ichigo the truth behind the deputy badge. However, even after learning the Soul Society's plans for him, Ichigo chooses to continue protecting his friends and defeats Ginjo.

Ichigo is sent back to the World of the Living by Squad Zero member Oh-Etsu Nimaiya, and there he learns about his past from Isshin. After finally learning the truth, Ichigo returns to Oh-Etsu and faces off against Zangetsu once again.

BLEACH STORIES

URYU ISHIDA 
石田雨竜
イシダウリュウ

ユーハバッハ 
YHWACH

HASCHWALTH 
ハッシュヴァルト

BLEACH 61
THE LAST 9DAYS

CONTENTS

541. THE BLADE AND ME 2 ——— 7
542. THE BLADE IS ME ——— 25
543. LETTERS ——— 43
544. WALKING WITH WATCHERS ——— 61
545. BLUE STRIPES ——— 79
546. THE LAST 9DAYS ——— 97
547. PEACE FROM SHADOWS ——— 115
548. THE THIN ICE ——— 137
549. THE STORMBRINGER ——— 155
550. BLAZING BULLETS ——— 173

541. THE BLADE AND ME 2

I TRIED NOT TO THINK ABOUT IT.

THAT DAY...

...WHEN I FIRST STOOD FACE TO FACE WITH HIM.

IT FELT LIKE I WAS DRAWN THERE.

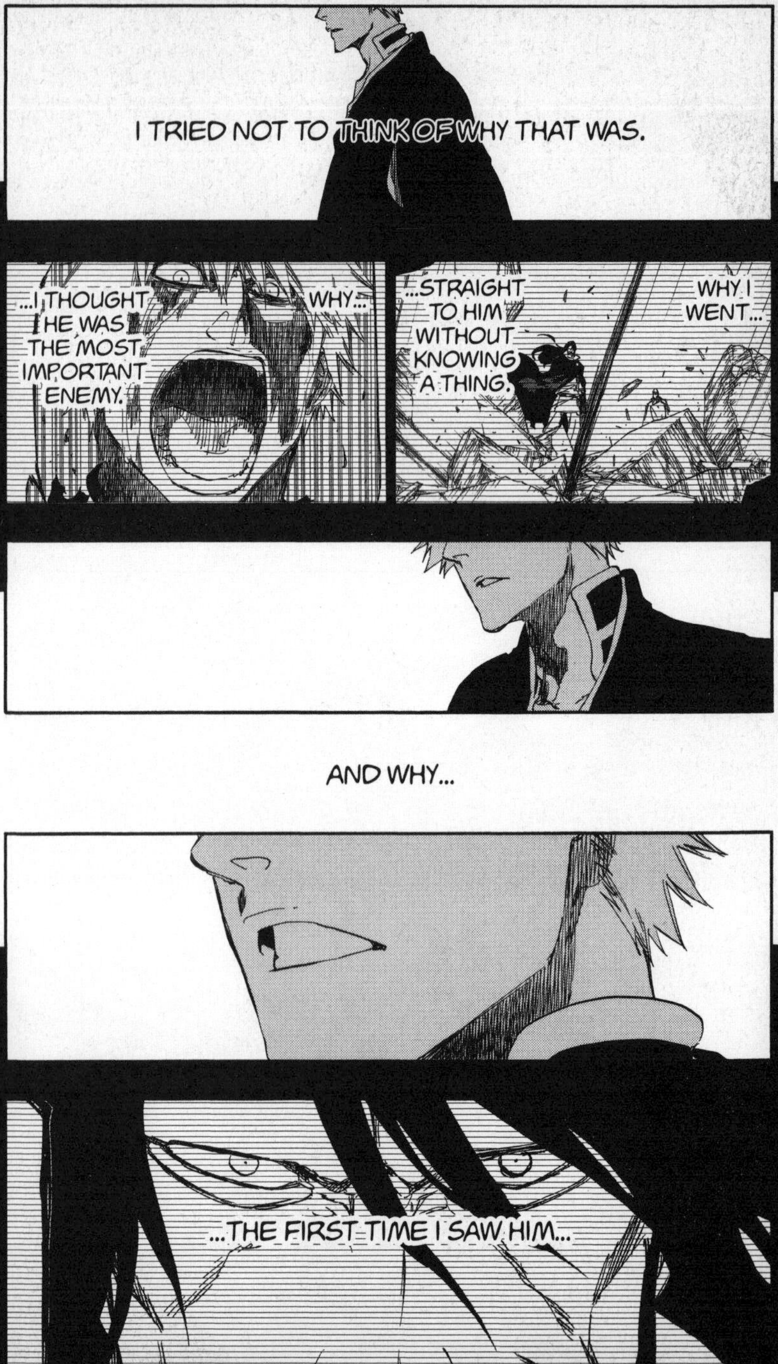
I TRIED NOT TO THINK OF WHY THAT WAS.
WHY I WENT...
...STRAIGHT TO HIM WITHOUT KNOWING A THING.
WHY...
...I THOUGHT HE WAS THE MOST IMPORTANT ENEMY.
AND WHY...
...THE FIRST TIME I SAW HIM...

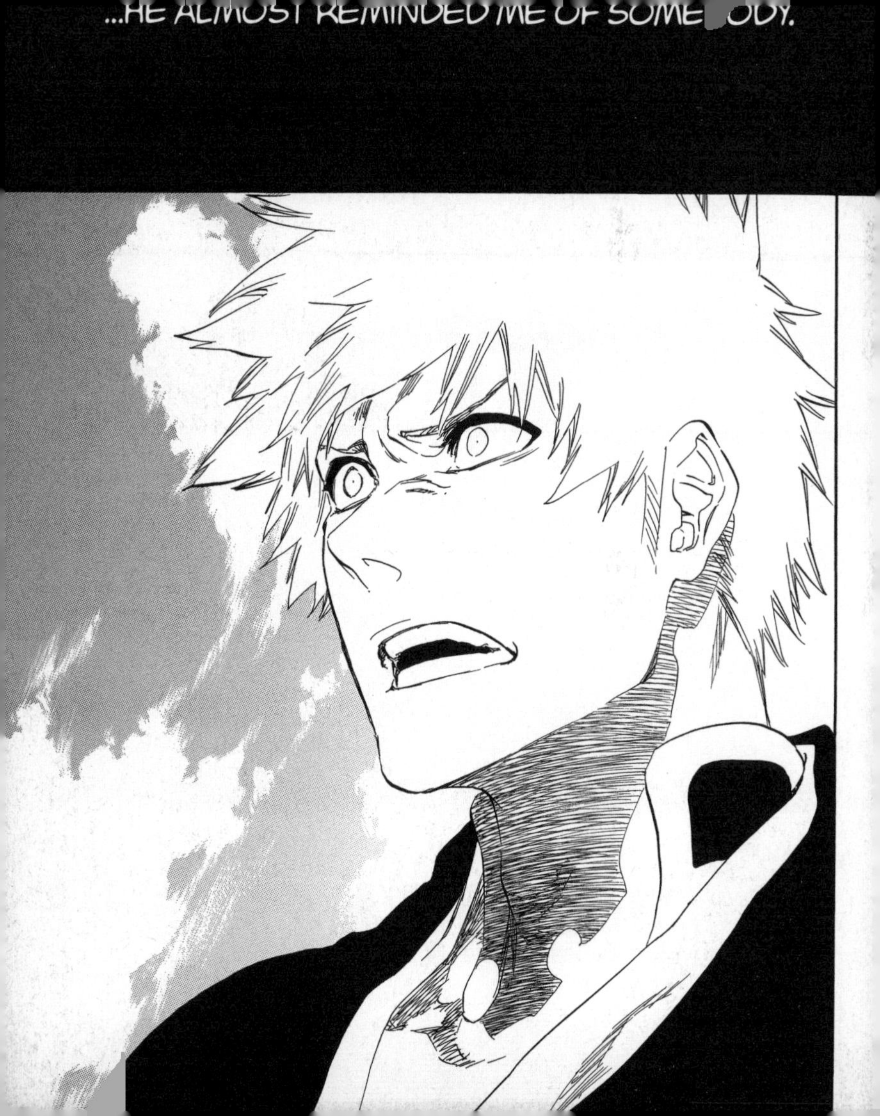
...HE ALMOST REMINDED ME OF SOME ODY.

ZANGETSU!!

THE BLADE AND ME 2

BLEACH 541.

...ZAN-GETSU?

WHY...

IT'S AS YOU WERE JUST TOLD.

AND...

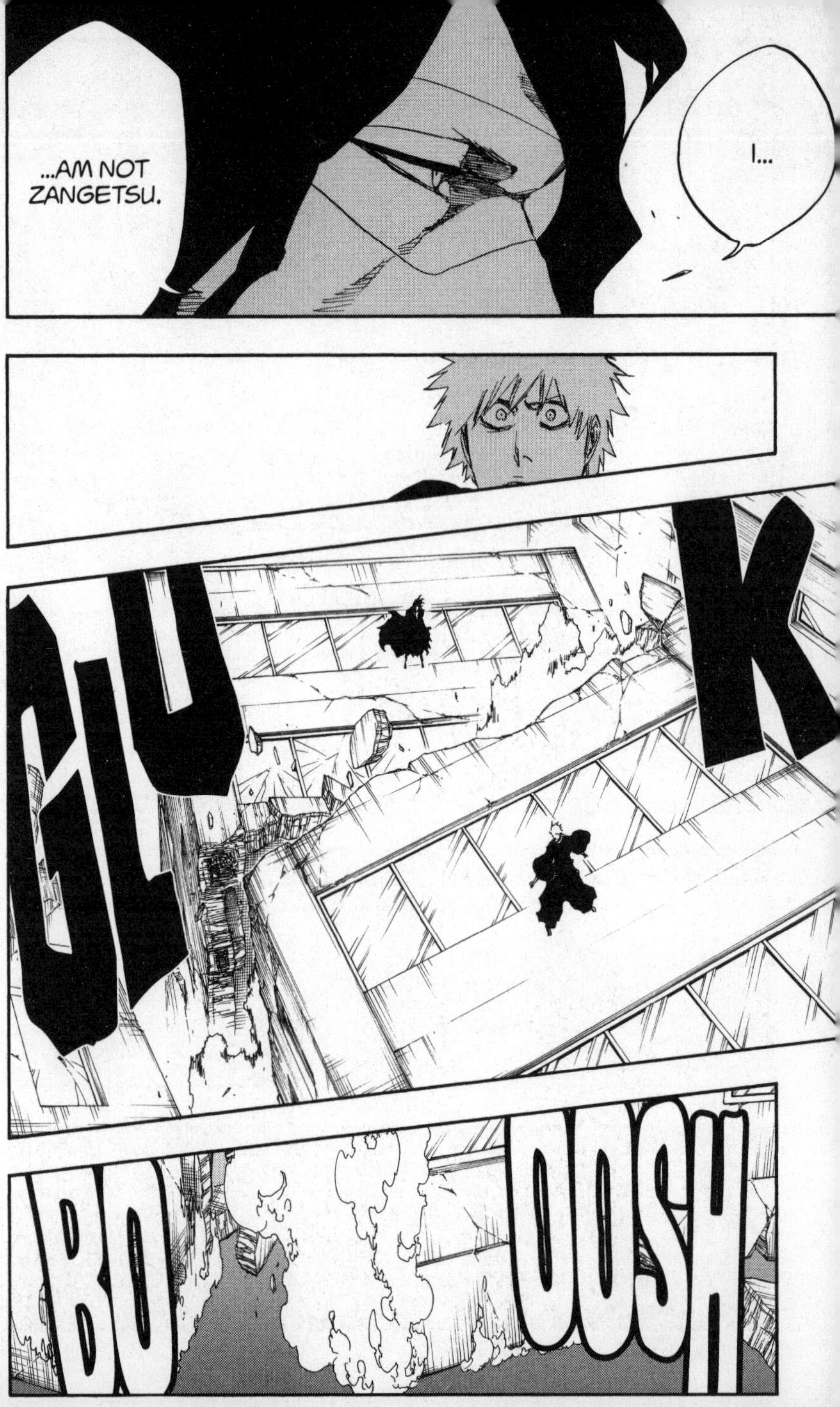
I...
...AM NOT ZANGETSU.
GU K
BO OOSH

ARE YOU REALLY...
... YHWACH ?
ARE YOU REALLY...
...NOT ZAN-GETSU ?
I AM...
...THE SOURCE OF THE QUINCY POWER INSIDE YOU.
I AM YHWACH AND I AM NOT YHWACH.
I DON'T UNDER-STAND !!
ARE YOU MY ENEMY ?!
OR ARE YOU MY FRIEND ?!
WAS EVERY-THING YOU SAID TO ME A LIE ?!

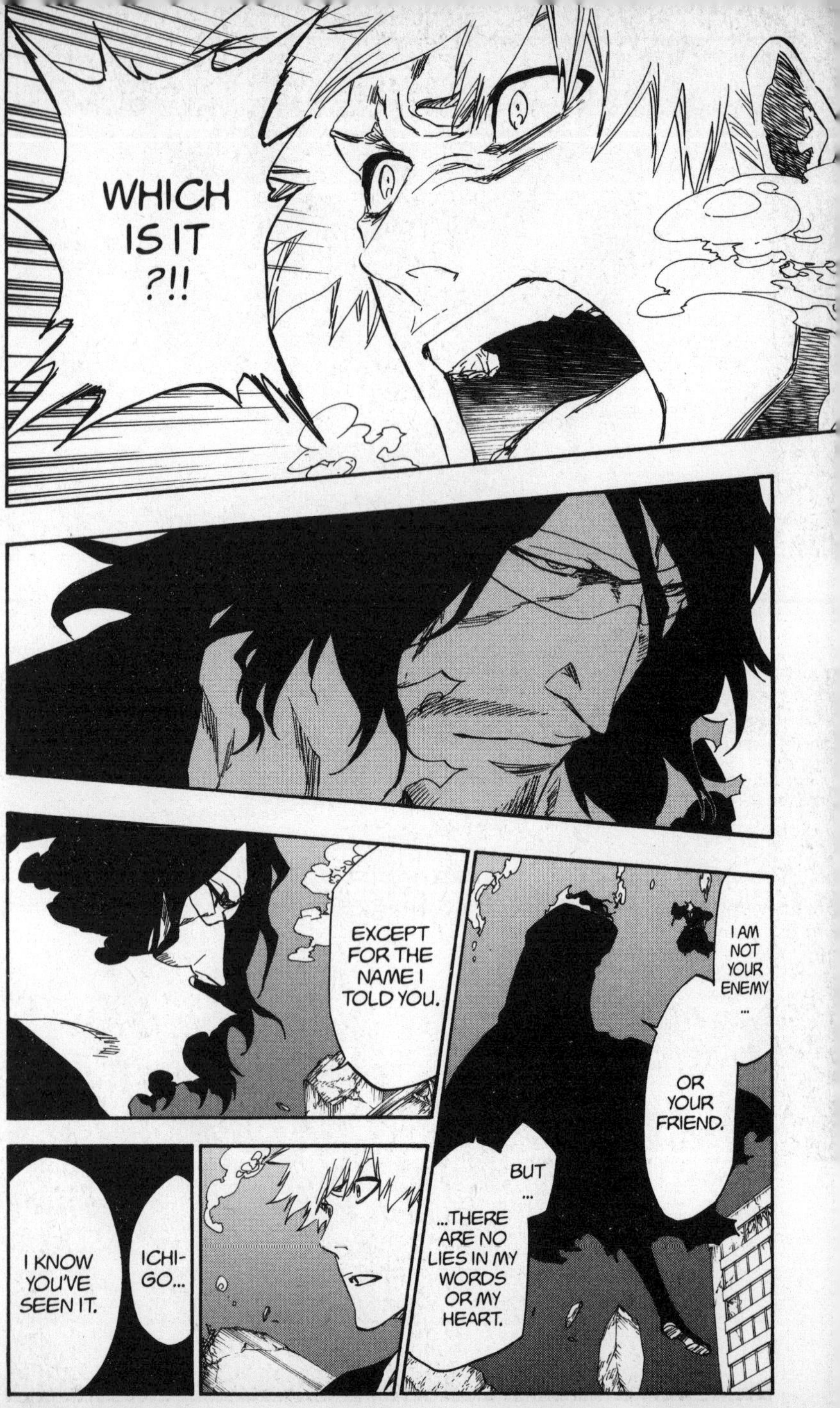
WHICH IS IT ?!!
I AM NOT YOUR ENEMY ...
OR YOUR FRIEND.
BUT ...
...THERE ARE NO LIES IN MY WORDS OR MY HEART.
EXCEPT FOR THE NAME I TOLD YOU.
ICHI-GO...
I KNOW YOU'VE SEEN IT.

READ THIS WAY

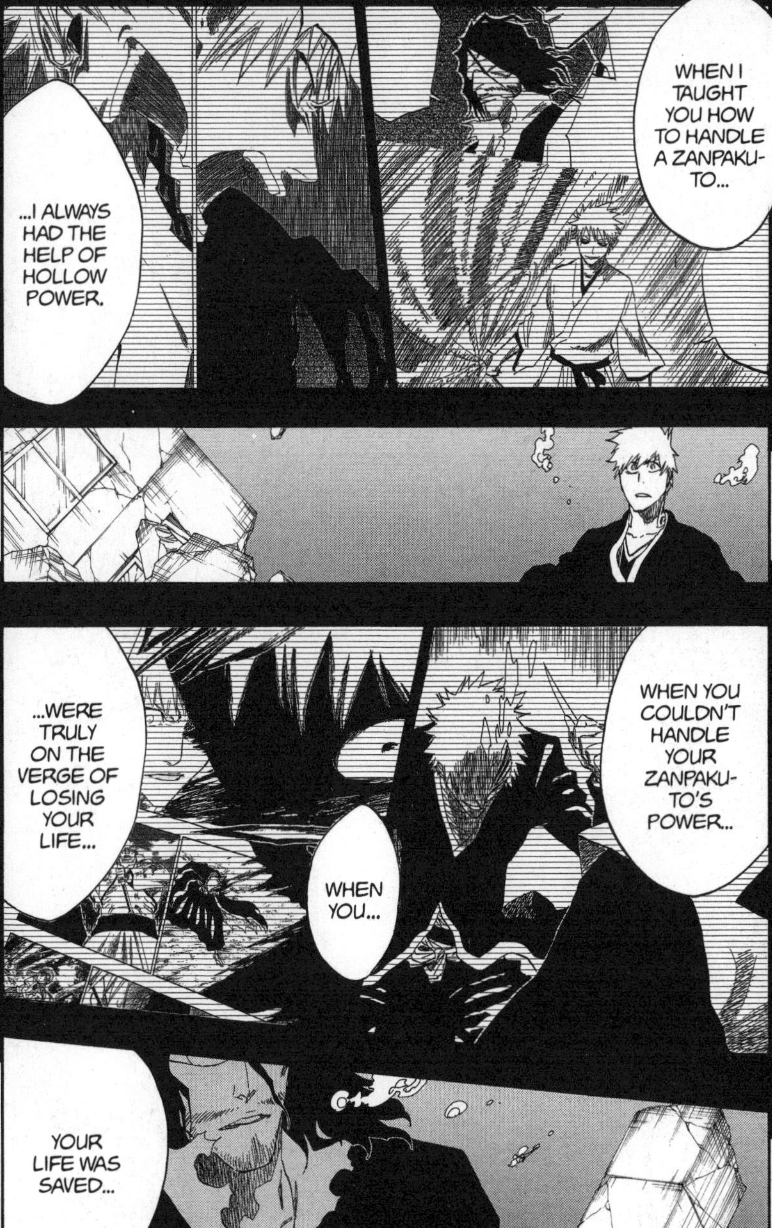

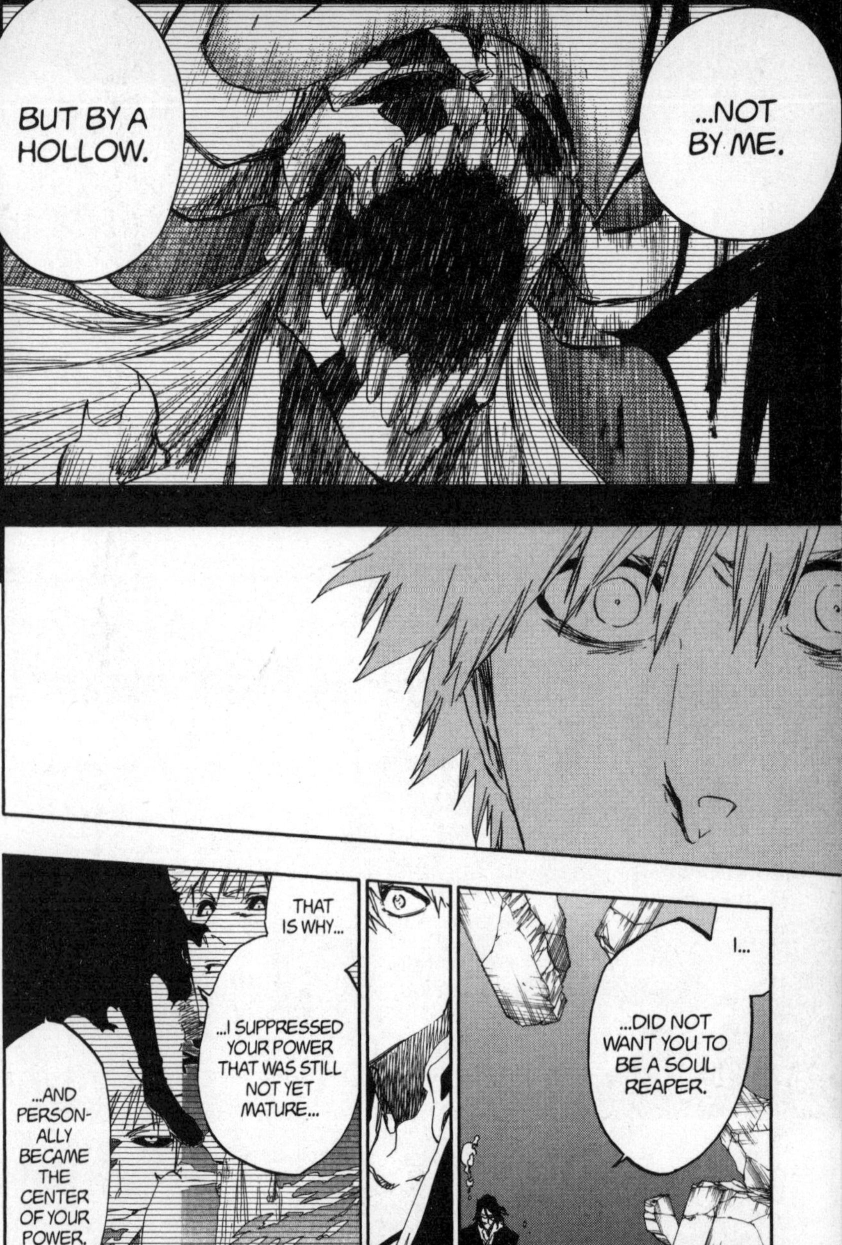
...NOT BY ME.
BUT BY A HOLLOW.
I...
...DID NOT WANT YOU TO BE A SOUL REAPER.
THAT IS WHY...
...I SUPPRESSED YOUR POWER THAT WAS STILL NOT YET MATURE...
...AND PERSON-ALLY BECAME THE CENTER OF YOUR POWER.

"WHY"?

WHAT IS THERE TO QUESTION...

...ABOUT WANTING TO KEEP YOU FAR AWAY FROM DANGER, FROM CONFLICT?

WHY...?

YOU WOULD SUFFER.

YOU WOULD BE HURT.

...YOU WOULD HAVE BEEN DRAGGED INTO BATTLE WHETHER YOU WANTED TO OR NOT.

IF YOU HAD BECOME A SOUL REAPER...

...I WOULD HAVE TO KILL YOU MYSELF.

AND EVENTUALLY...

BOOO

GRP

WOOSH...

IF YOU BECAME ONE, I WOULD HAVE TO KILL YOU.

I COULD NOT LET YOU BE A SOUL REAPER.

THAT IS WHAT I THOUGHT...

...YOU TRAVELED DOWN THAT PATH WITH YOUR OWN FREE WILL. THROUGH PAIN AND SUFFERING... YOU STRENGTHENED YOURSELF. YOU WERE GIVEN AN OPPORTUNITY.

HOWEVER... ...YOU CHOSE THE PATH OF A SOUL REAPER.

...NOW I...

AND...

EVENTUALLY... ...MY WISH OF KEEPING YOU FAR AWAY FROM SOUL REAPERS... ...TILTED TOWARD HELPING YOUR DECISION.

AS I WATCHED YOU... ...I COULD ALMOST HEAR MY HEART WAVERING.

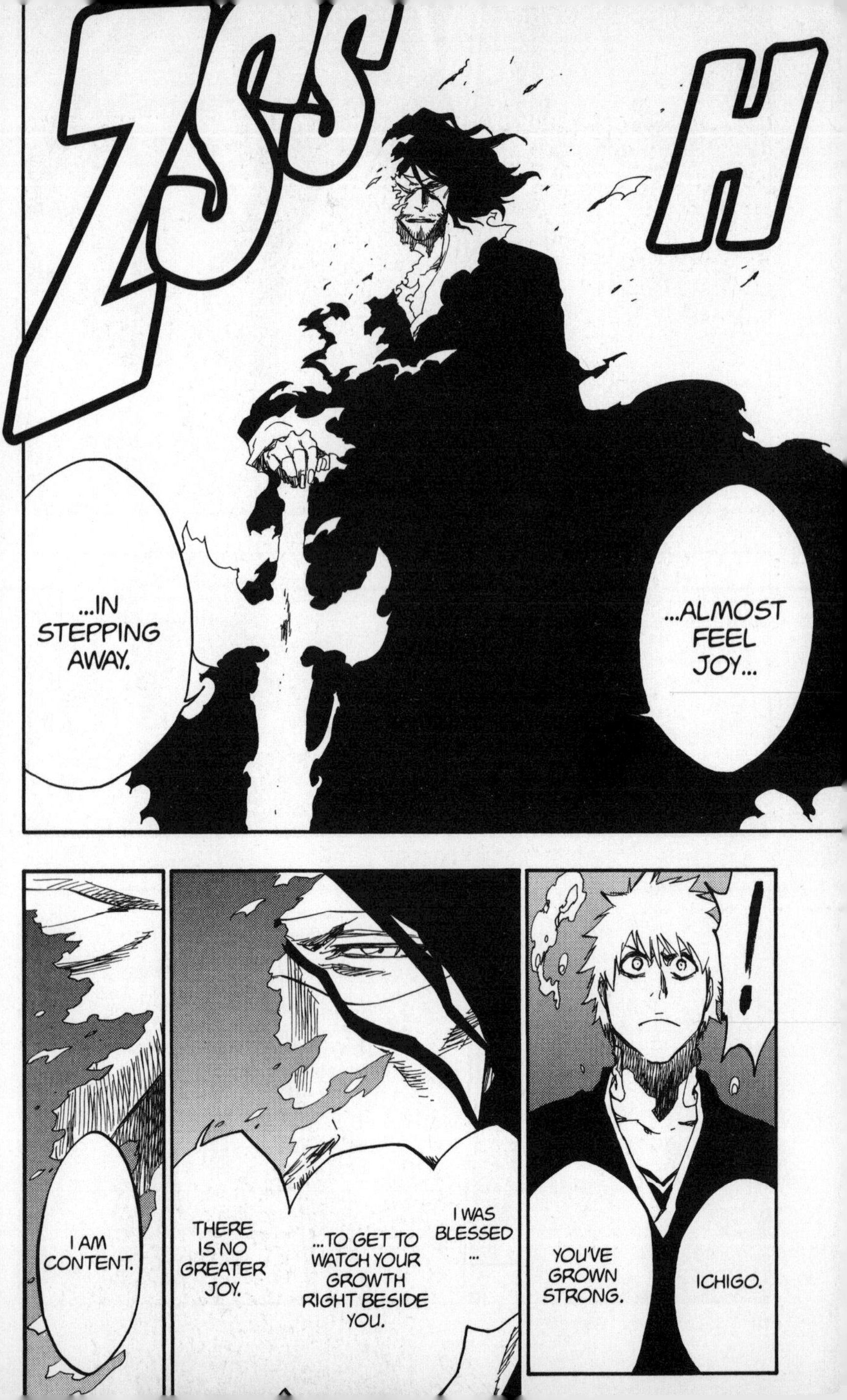
ZSSH
...ALMOST FEEL JOY...
...IN STEPPING AWAY.
ICHIGO.
YOU'VE GROWN STRONG.
I WAS BLESSED ...
...TO GET TO WATCH YOUR GROWTH RIGHT BESIDE YOU.
THERE IS NO GREATER JOY.
I AM CONTENT.

READ THIS WAY

W...
WAIT, ZANGETSU !!
I STILL HAVEN'T ...

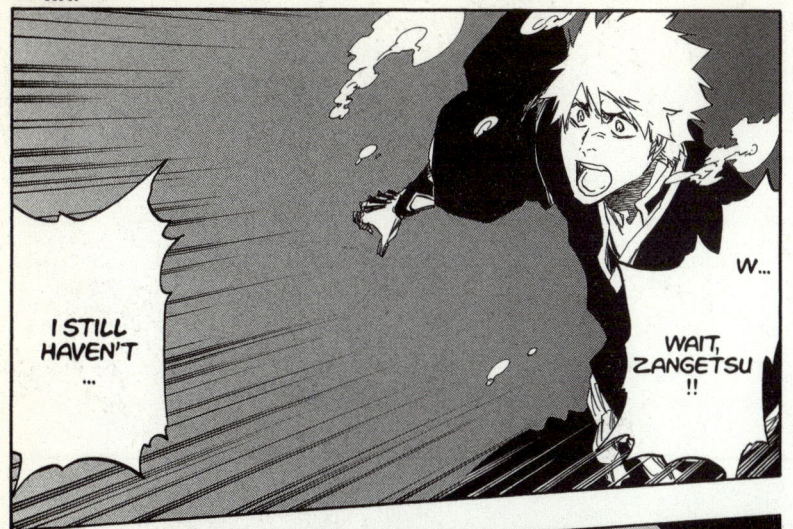

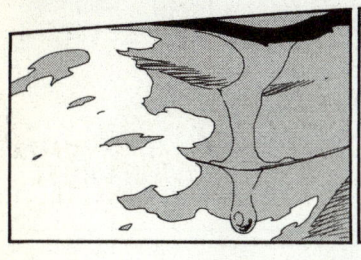

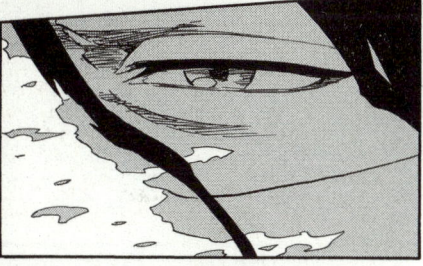

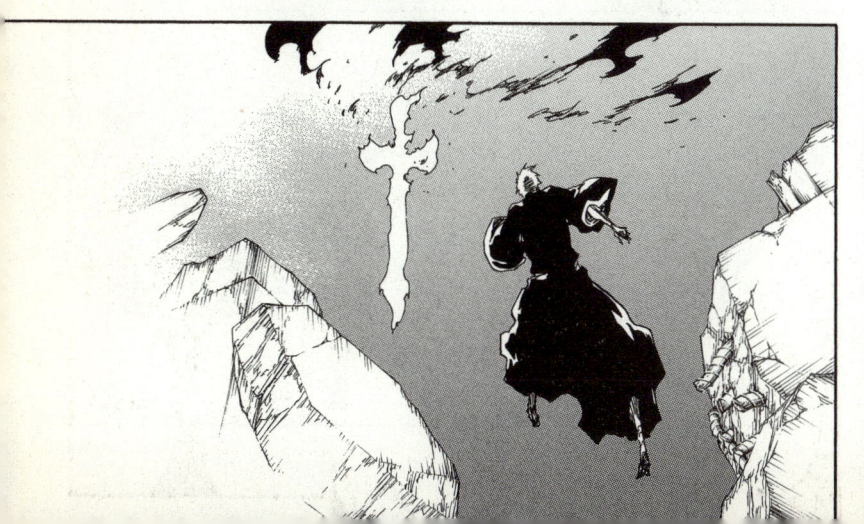

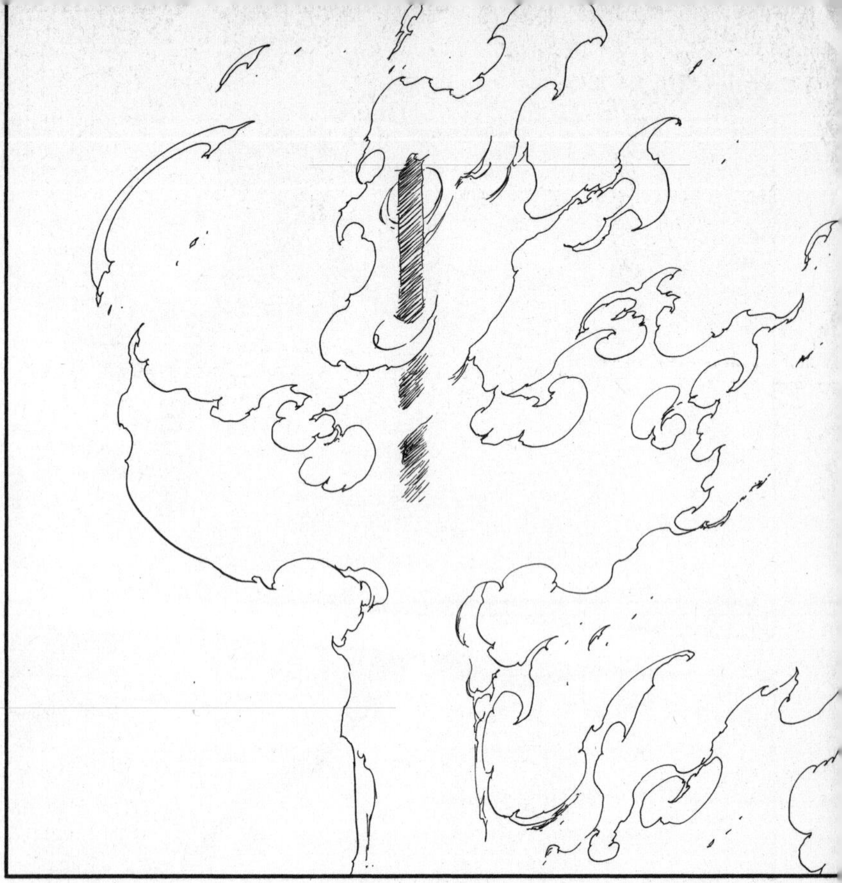
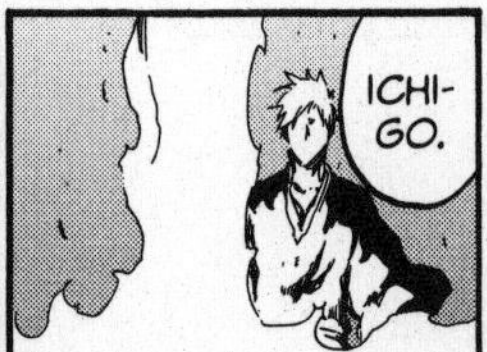
ICHI-GO.
WHAT YOU'VE BEEN USING ...
...IS MERELY A FRAGMENT OF YOUR POWER THAT I COULD NOT CONTAIN.
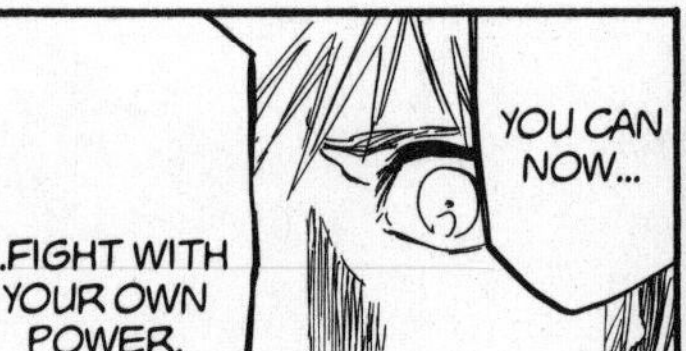
YOU CAN NOW...
...FIGHT WITH YOUR OWN POWER.
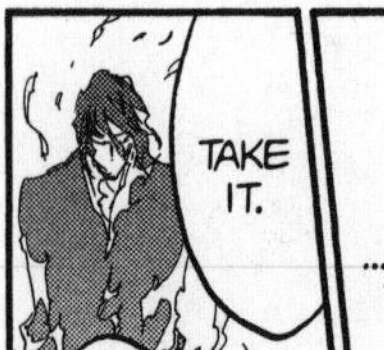
TAKE IT.
THAT IS YOUR TRUE ZANPAKU-TO...

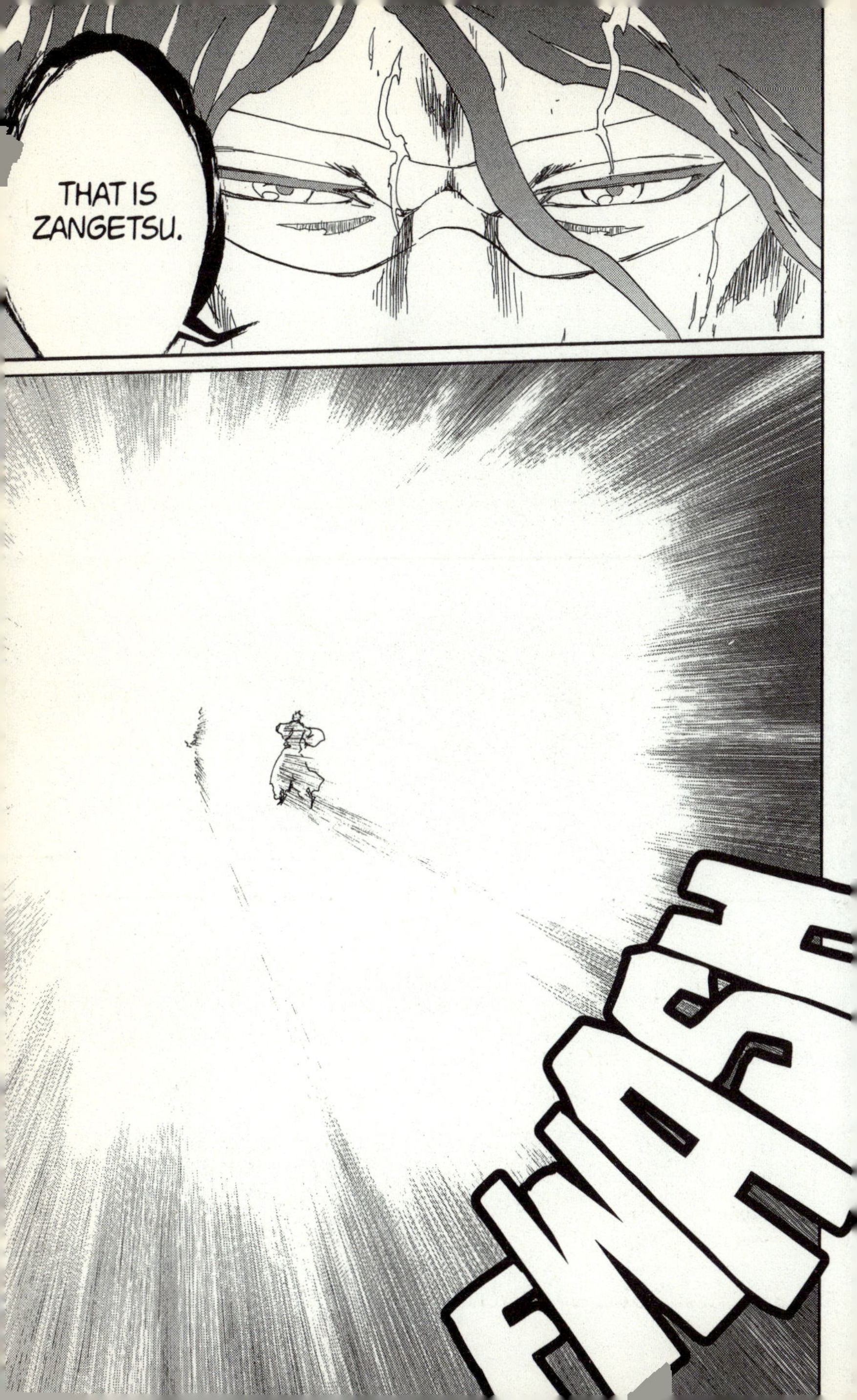
THAT IS ZANGETSU.

YEAH. THERE WERE NO LIES.
NOT IN HIS WORDS.
NOT IN YOURS EITHER.
YOU USED A QUINCY'S SHADOW TO HELP ME.
YOU USED A QUINCY'S BLOOD TO STOP MINE.
YOU LENT ME THE POWER OF A QUINCY...
...TO HELP ME BE STRONGER.

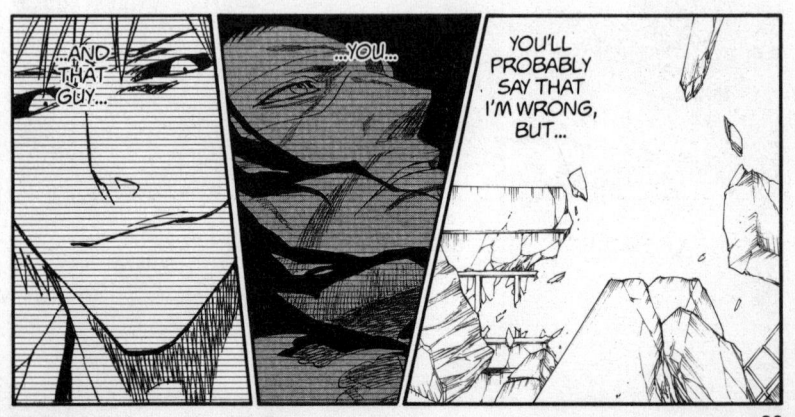

ZANGETSU.

I DON'T CARE WHO YOU ARE.

...AND THAT GUY...

...YOU...

YOU'LL PROBABLY SAY THAT I'M WRONG, BUT...

...ZANGETSU.

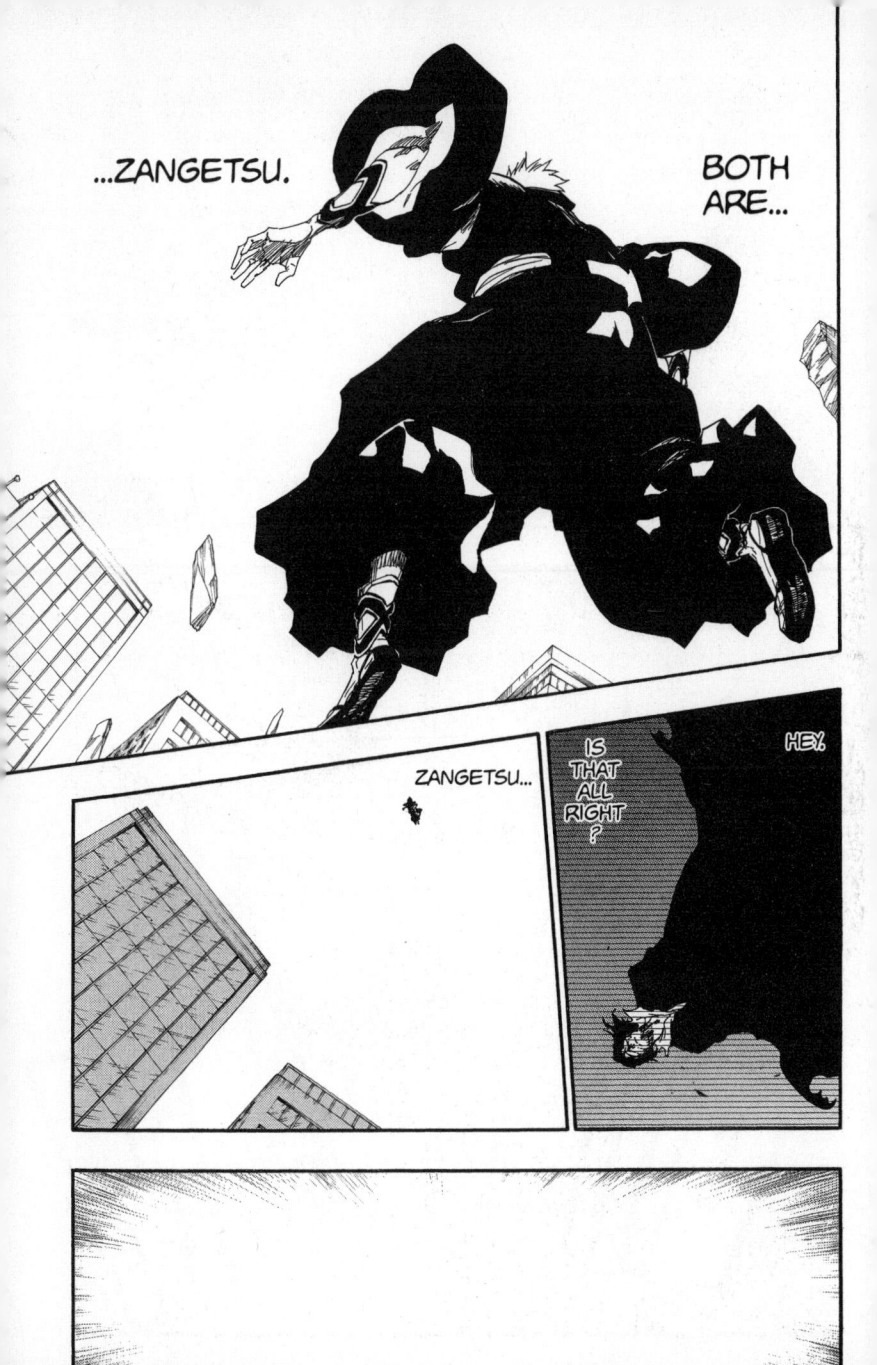

BOTH ARE...

ZANGETSU...

IS THAT ALL RIGHT?

HEY.

GWOOOF

DOOM

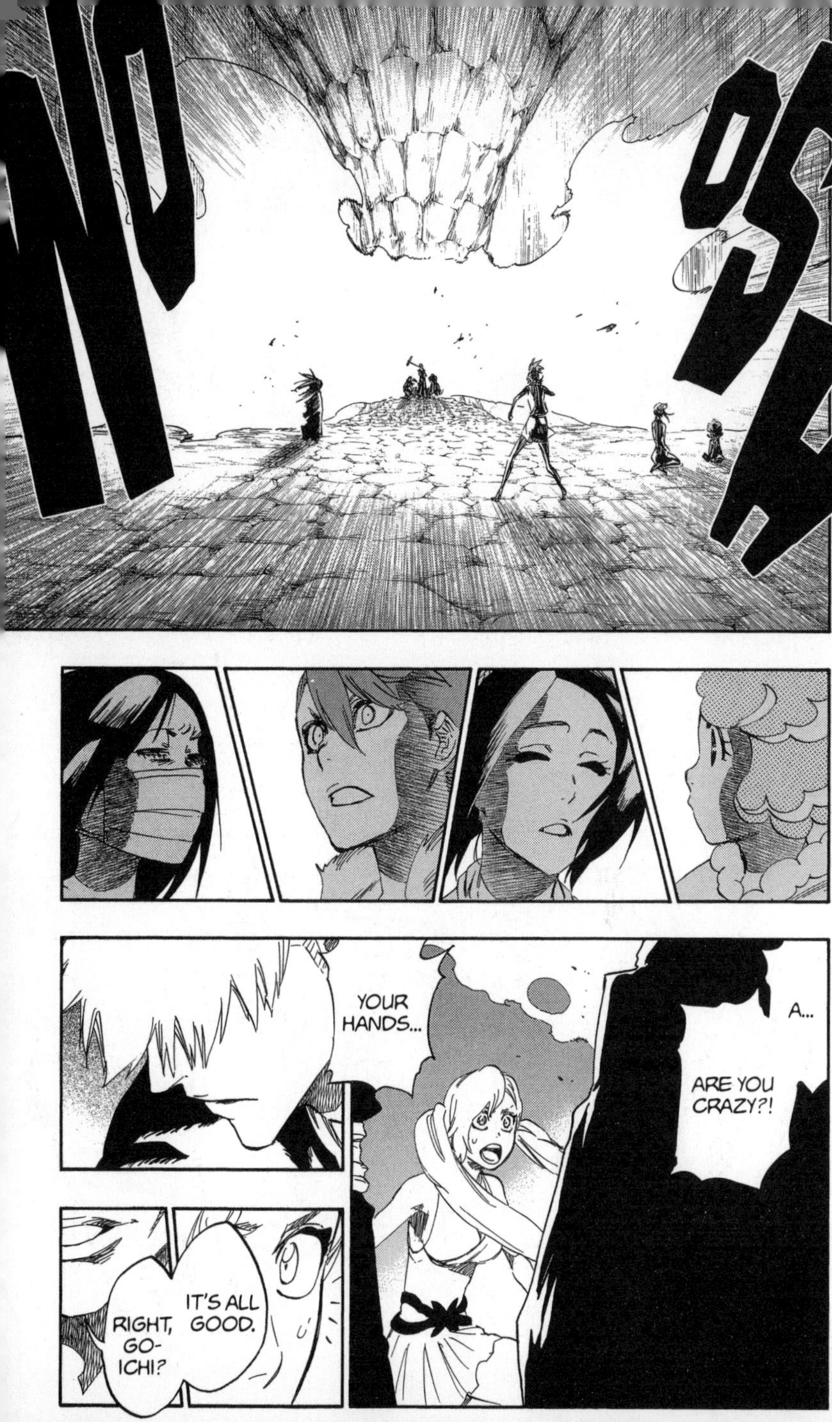
A...
ARE YOU CRAZY?!
YOUR HANDS...
IT'S ALL GOOD.
RIGHT, GO-ICHI?

...BEEN PUT INTO IT.

...YOUR SOUL'S...

...COMPLETE ONCE...

...IT'D BE...

I WAS JUST THINKING...

PULL IT OUT, GO-ICHI!

GO ON.

...IS YOUR ZANPAKU-TO!

THAT...

GRP...

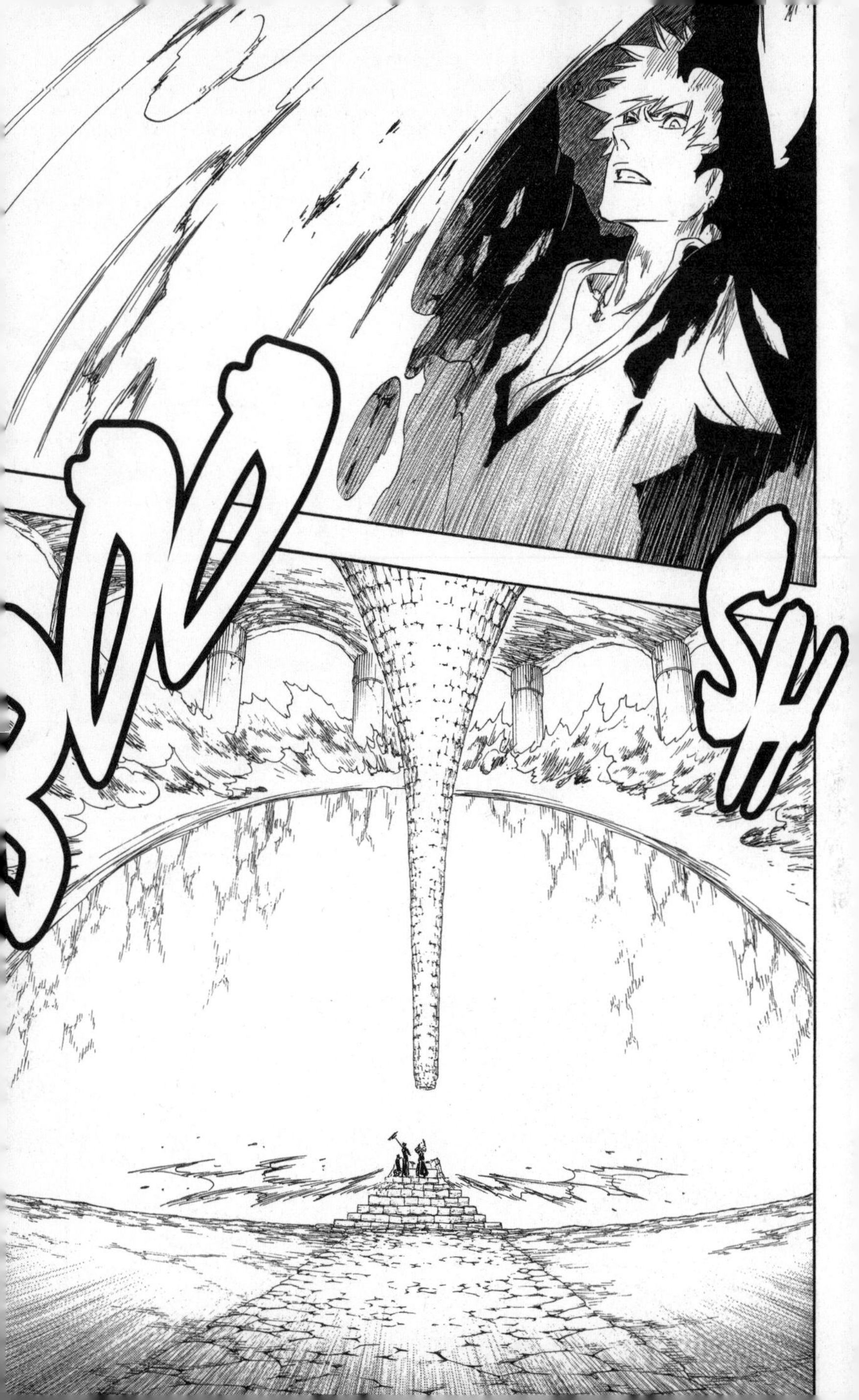

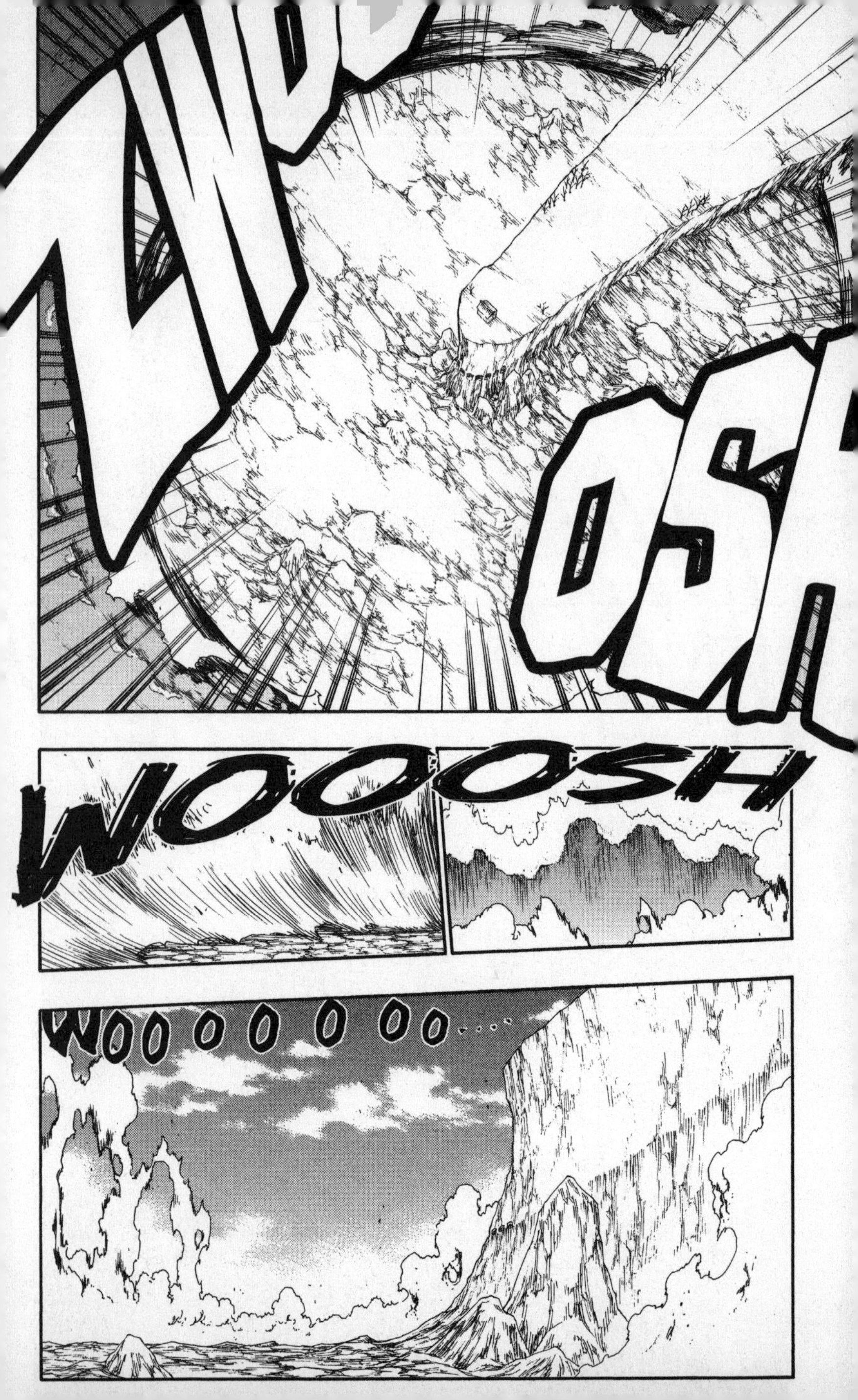
WOOOSH
WOOOOOOO...

Panel 1
HAVE YOU EVER SEEN ANYTHING LIKE THIS...?

HELL NO!

Panel 2
THE WATER'S GONE...!

...

Panel 3
THE SEA DRIED UP FROM THE HEAT AND SPIRITUAL PRESSURE.

IN ORDER TO COOL THE SOUL OF THE SWORD.

Panel 4
WHAT D'YOU THINK, GO-ICHI?

YOU THINK YOU CAN GET ALONG?

Panel 5
WITH...

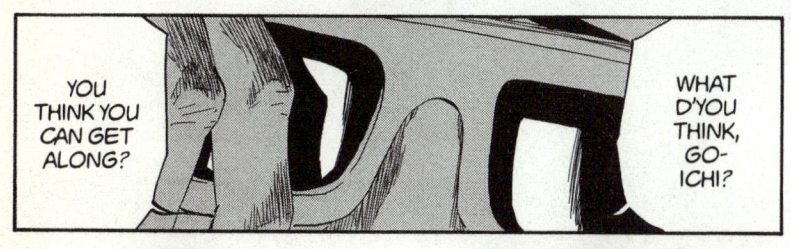

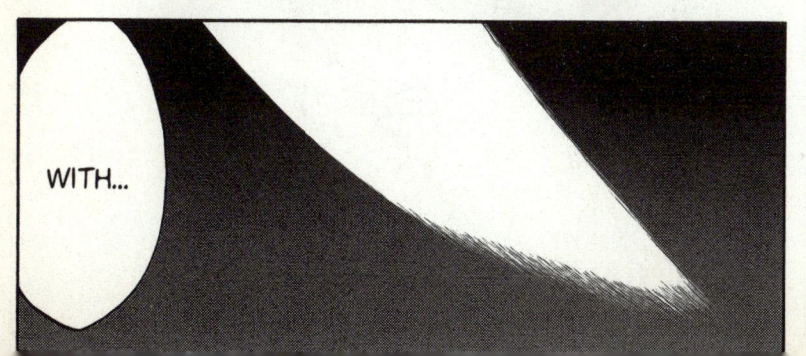

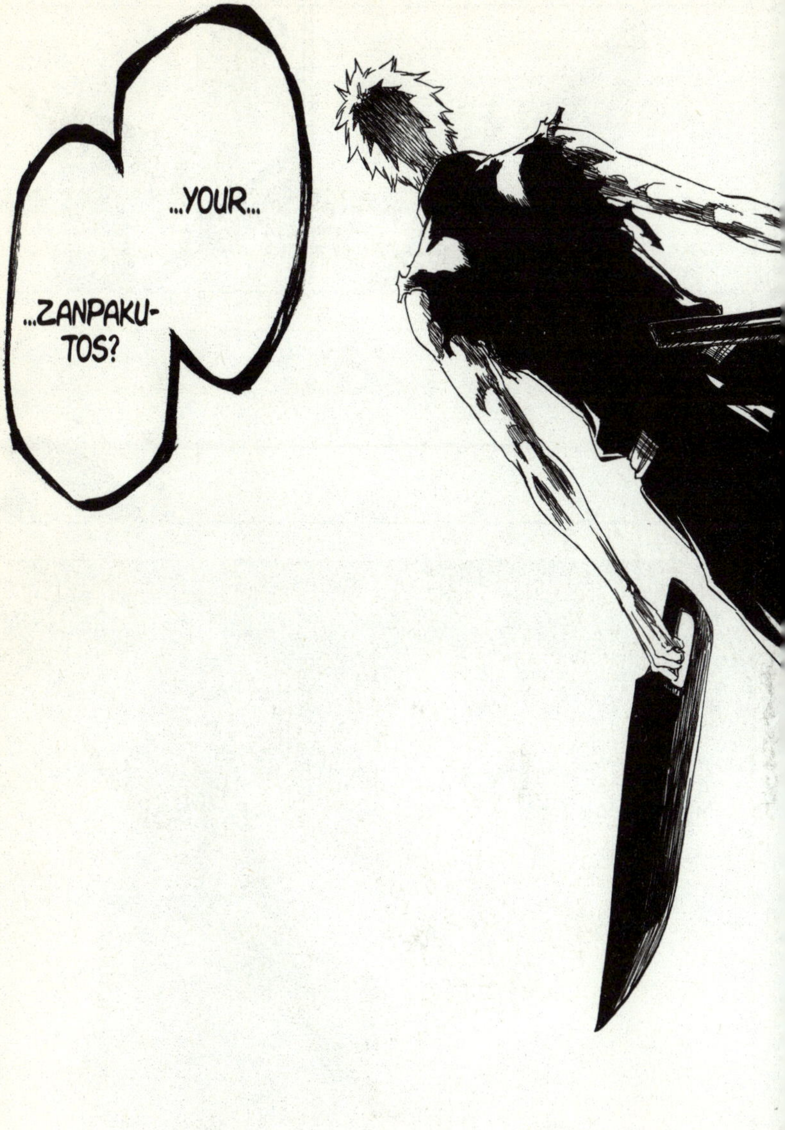
...YOUR...
...ZANPAKU-TOS?

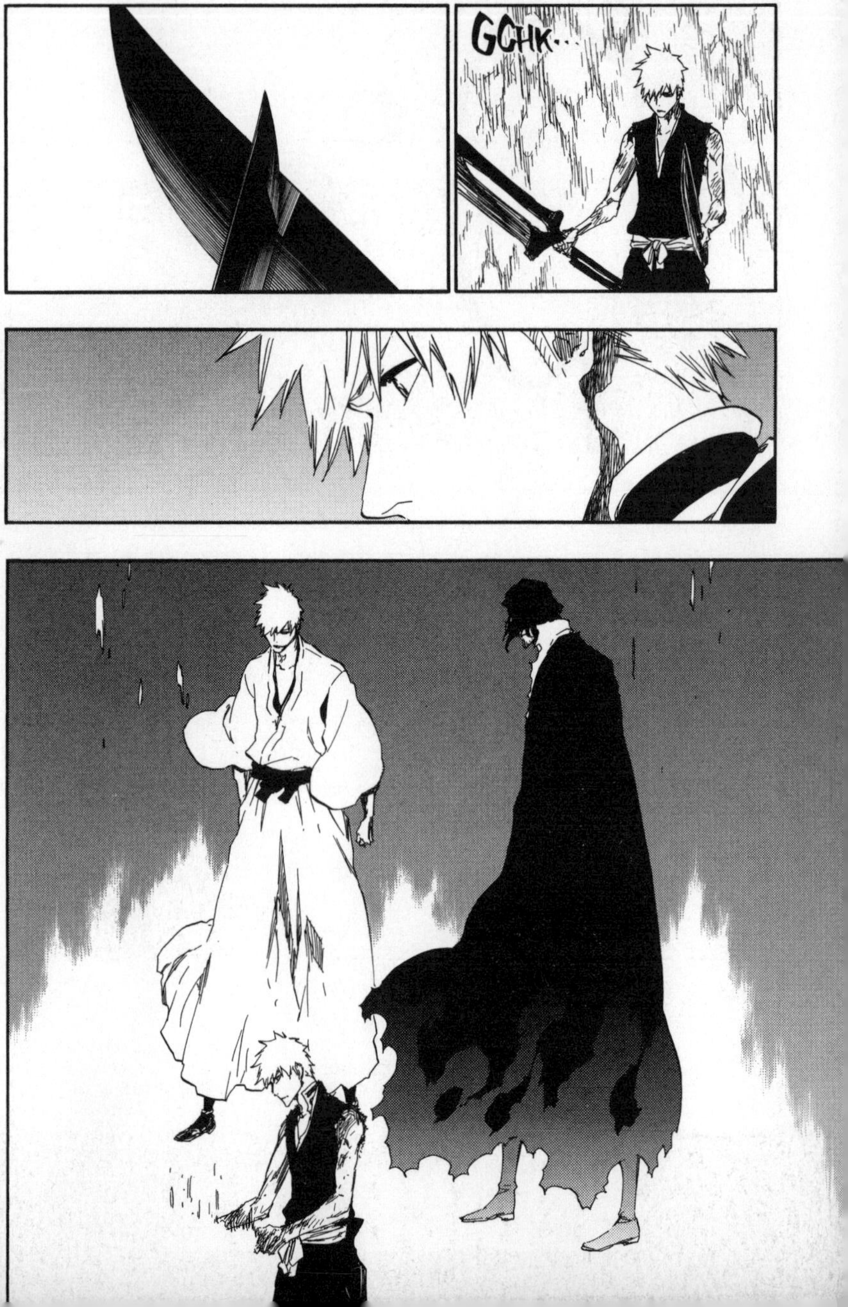
GCHK...

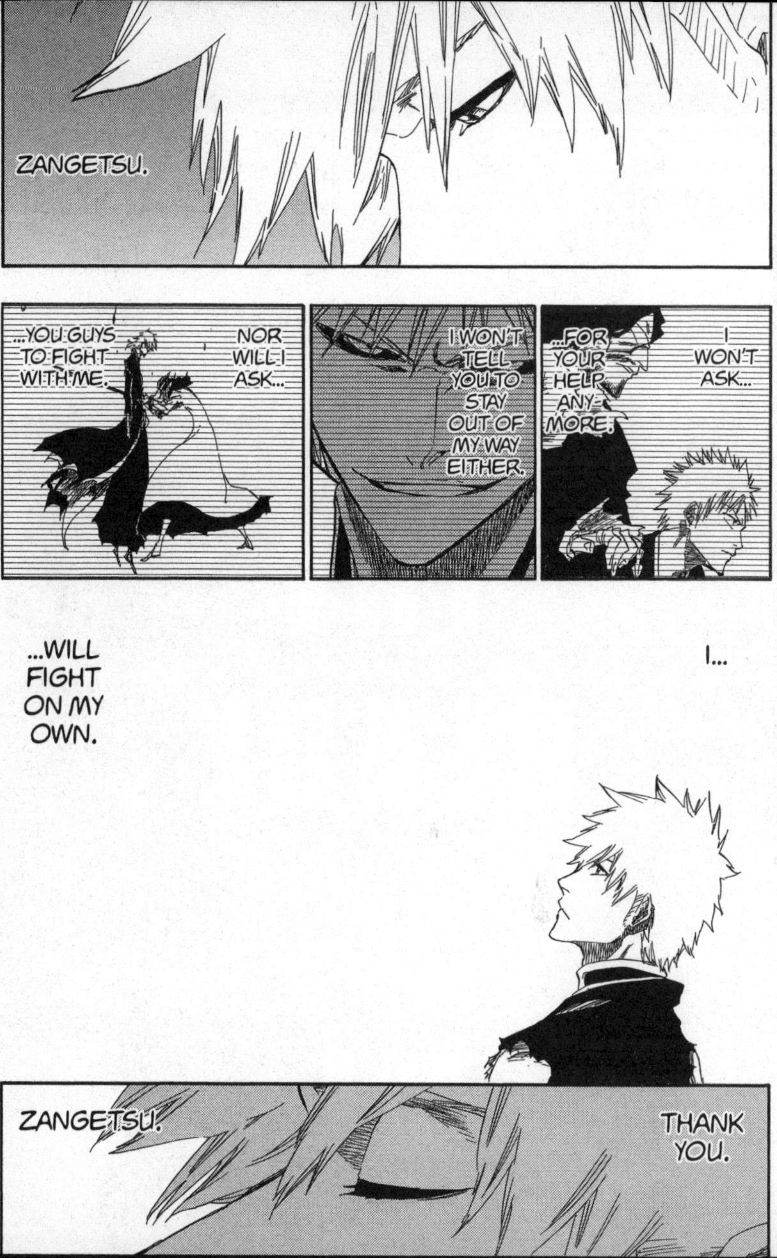
ZANGETSU.
I WON'T ASK...
...FOR YOUR HELP ANYMORE.
I WON'T TELL YOU TO STAY OUT OF MY WAY EITHER.
NOR WILL I ASK...
...YOU GUYS TO FIGHT WITH ME.
I...
...WILL FIGHT ON MY OWN.
THANK YOU.
ZANGETSU.

BLEACH 542.

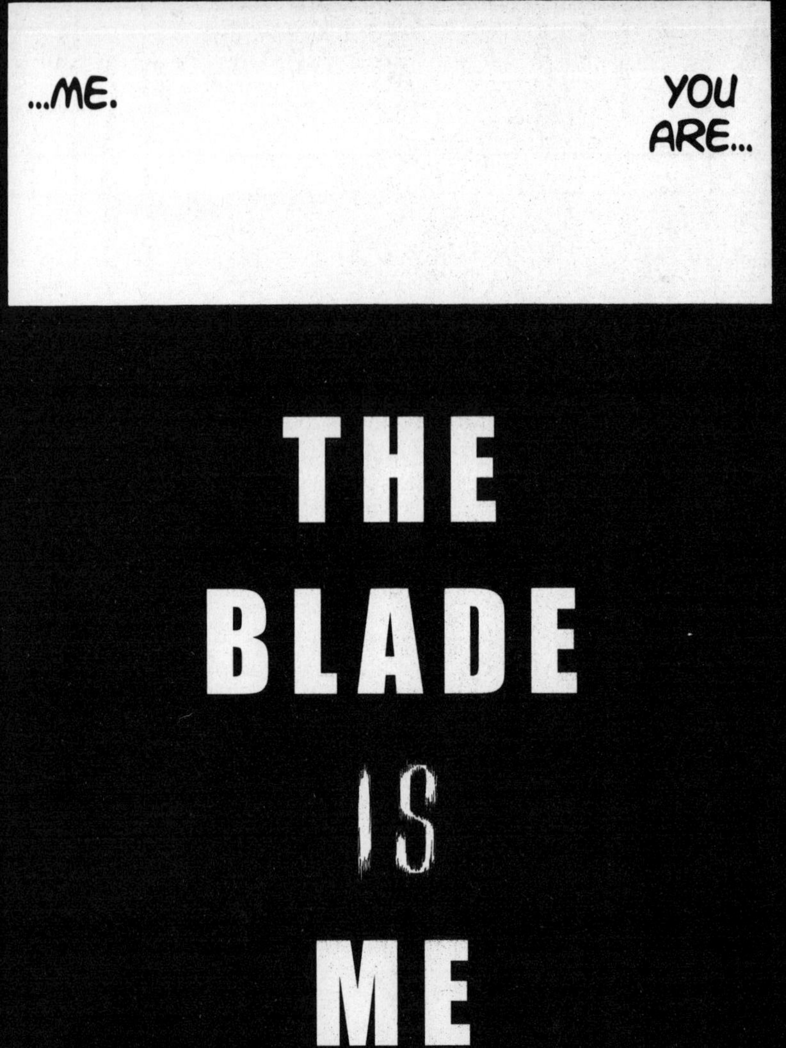
YOU ARE...
...ME.
THE BLADE IS ME

SHOOM

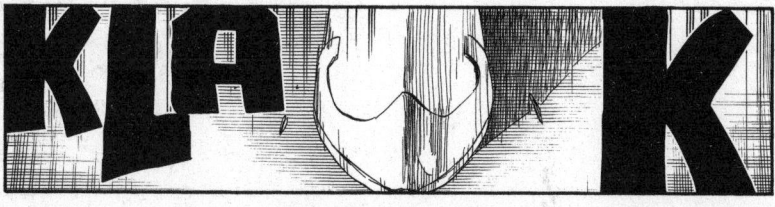

KLAK

KLAK KLAK KLAK KLAK KLAK KLAK

RAISE YOUR CROSSES!

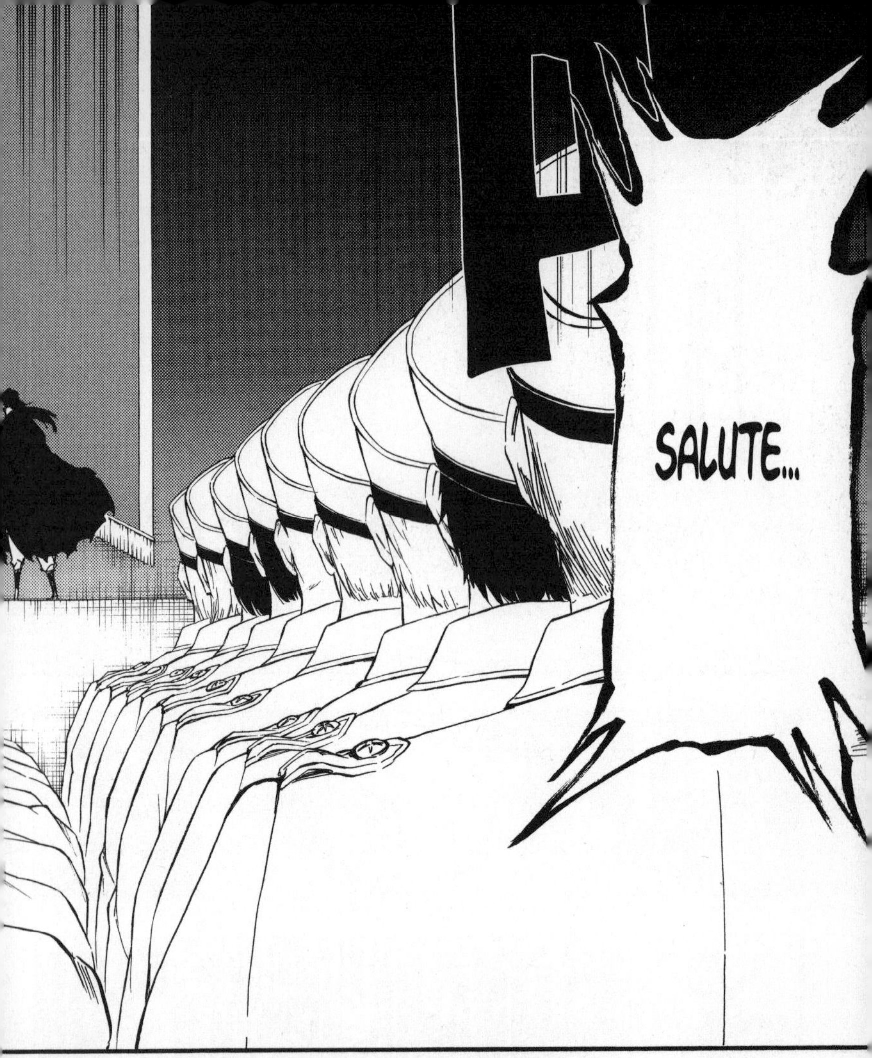
SALUTE...
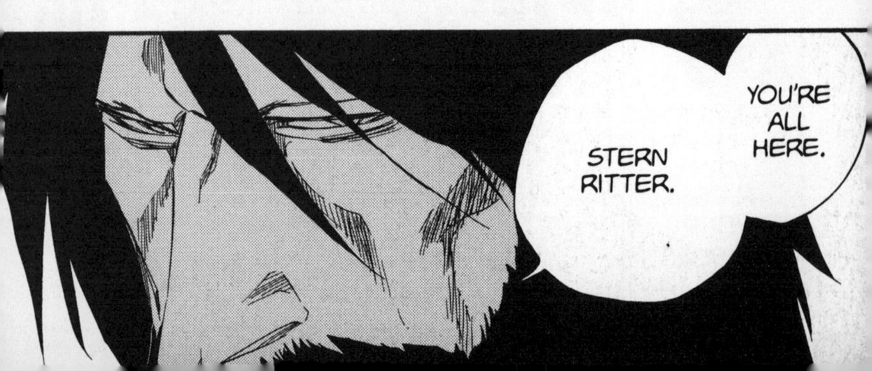
YOU'RE ALL HERE.
STERN RITTER.

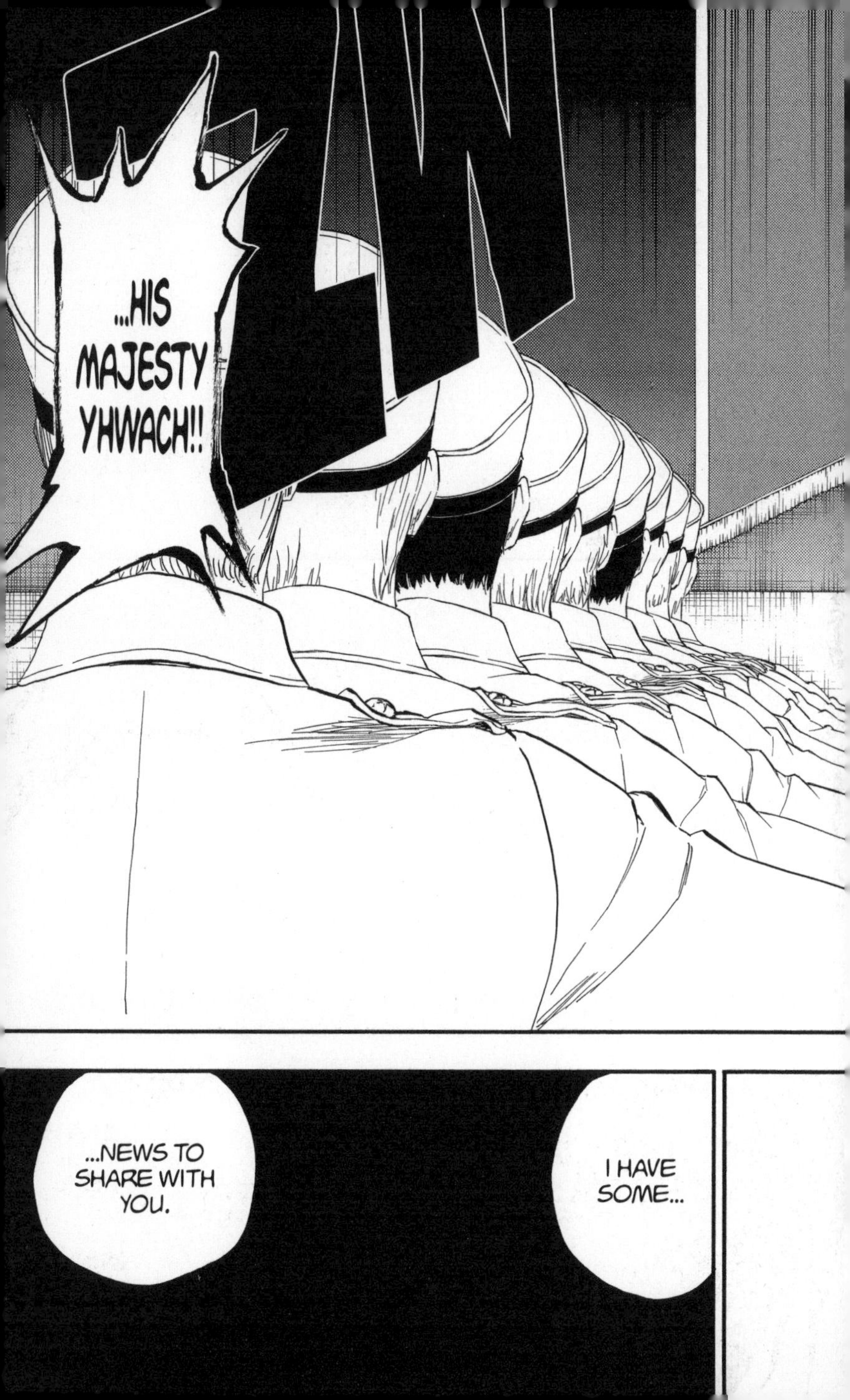
...HIS MAJESTY YHWACH!!
I HAVE SOME...
...NEWS TO SHARE WITH YOU.

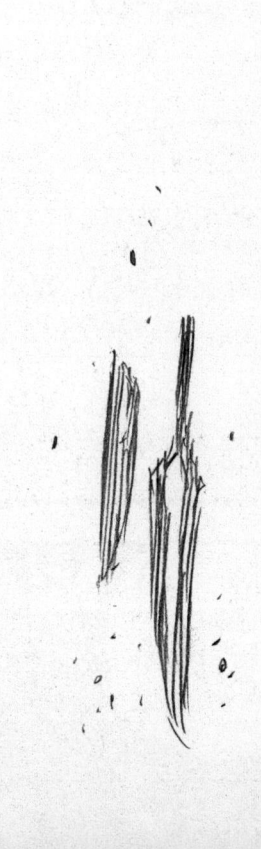

STERN RITTER.

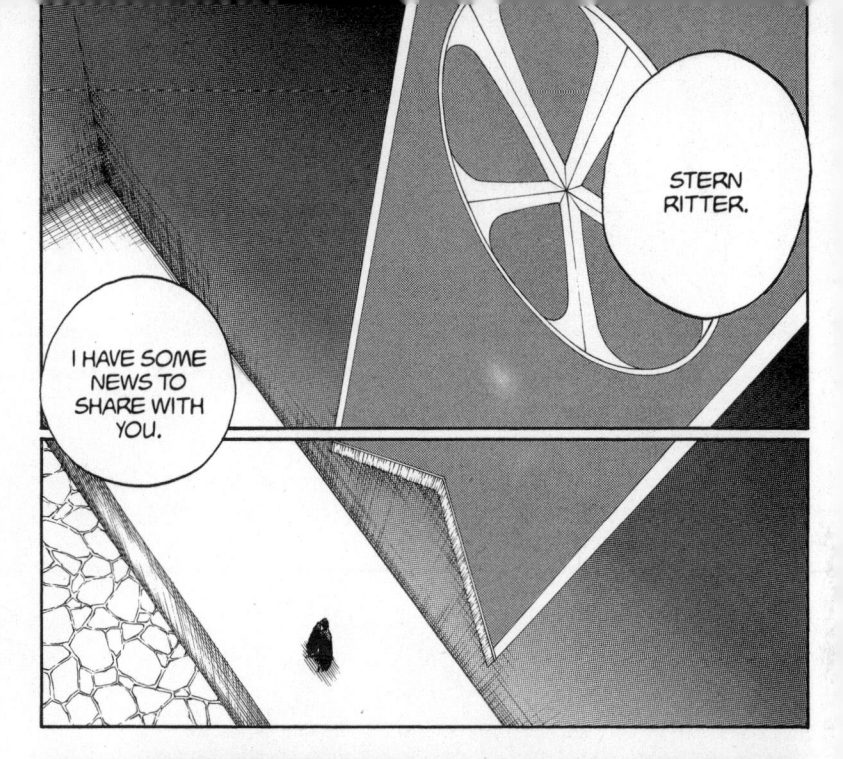

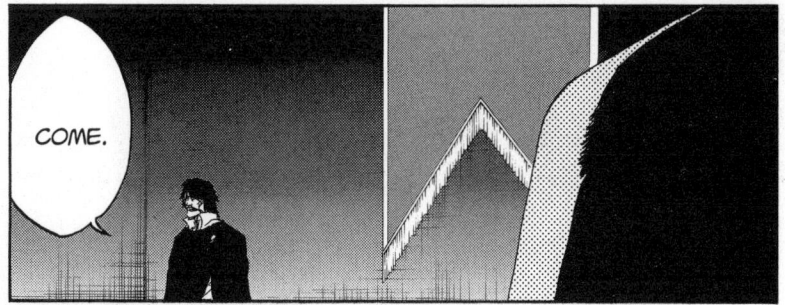

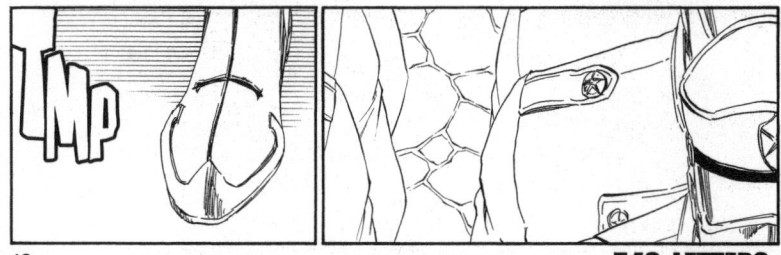

I HAVE SOME NEWS TO SHARE WITH YOU.

COME.

543. LETTERS

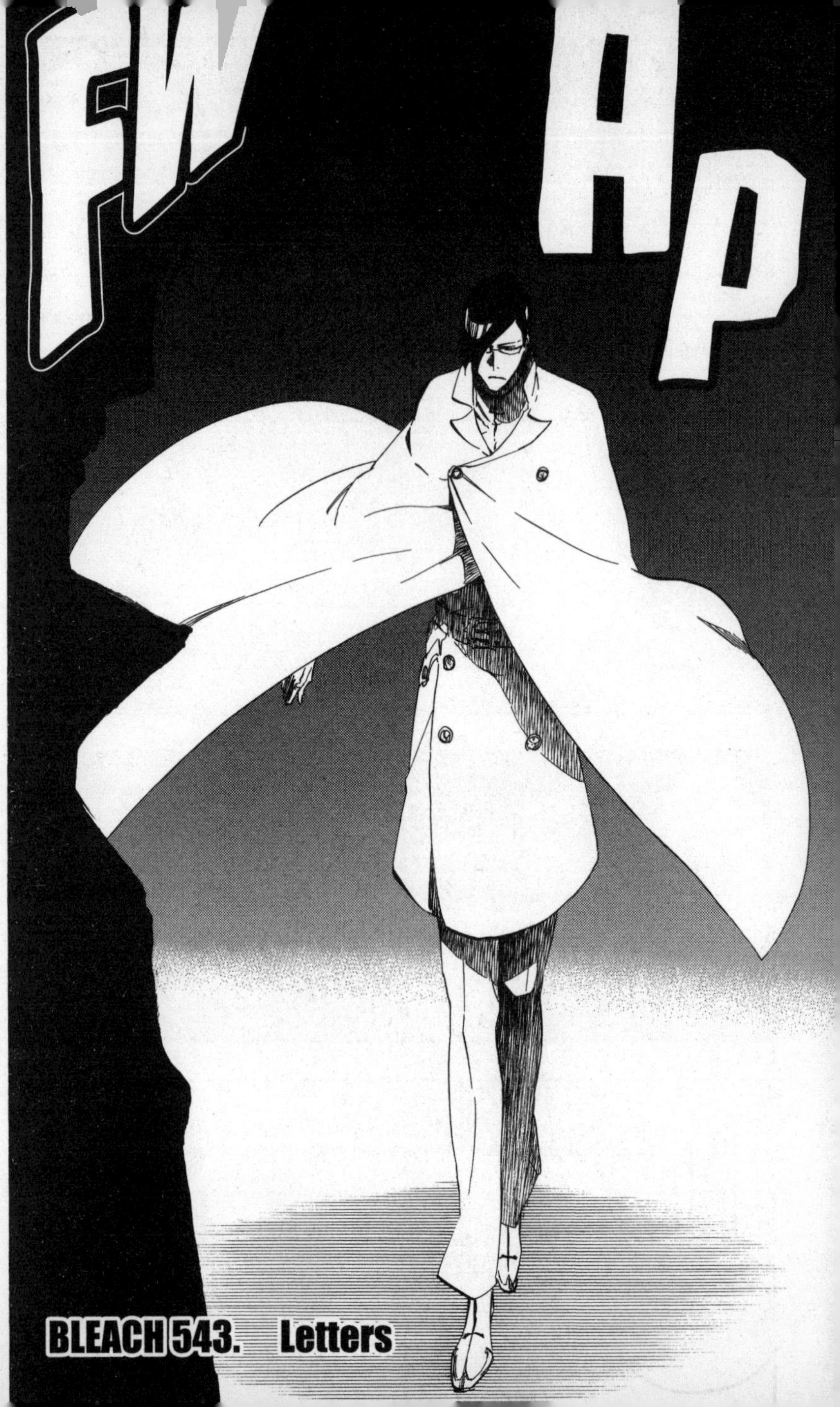
FWAP
BLEACH 543. Letters

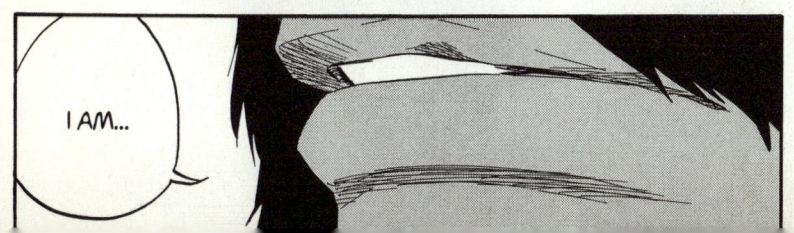

GASP

WHAT...?

MUTTER MUTTER MUTTER MUTTER

WHO IS THAT GUY...?!

WHY IS HE ON THE SAME STAGE AS HIS MAJESTY...?

URYU ISHIDA.

HE IS THE LAST SURVIVING QUINCY IN THIS WORLD.

I AM...

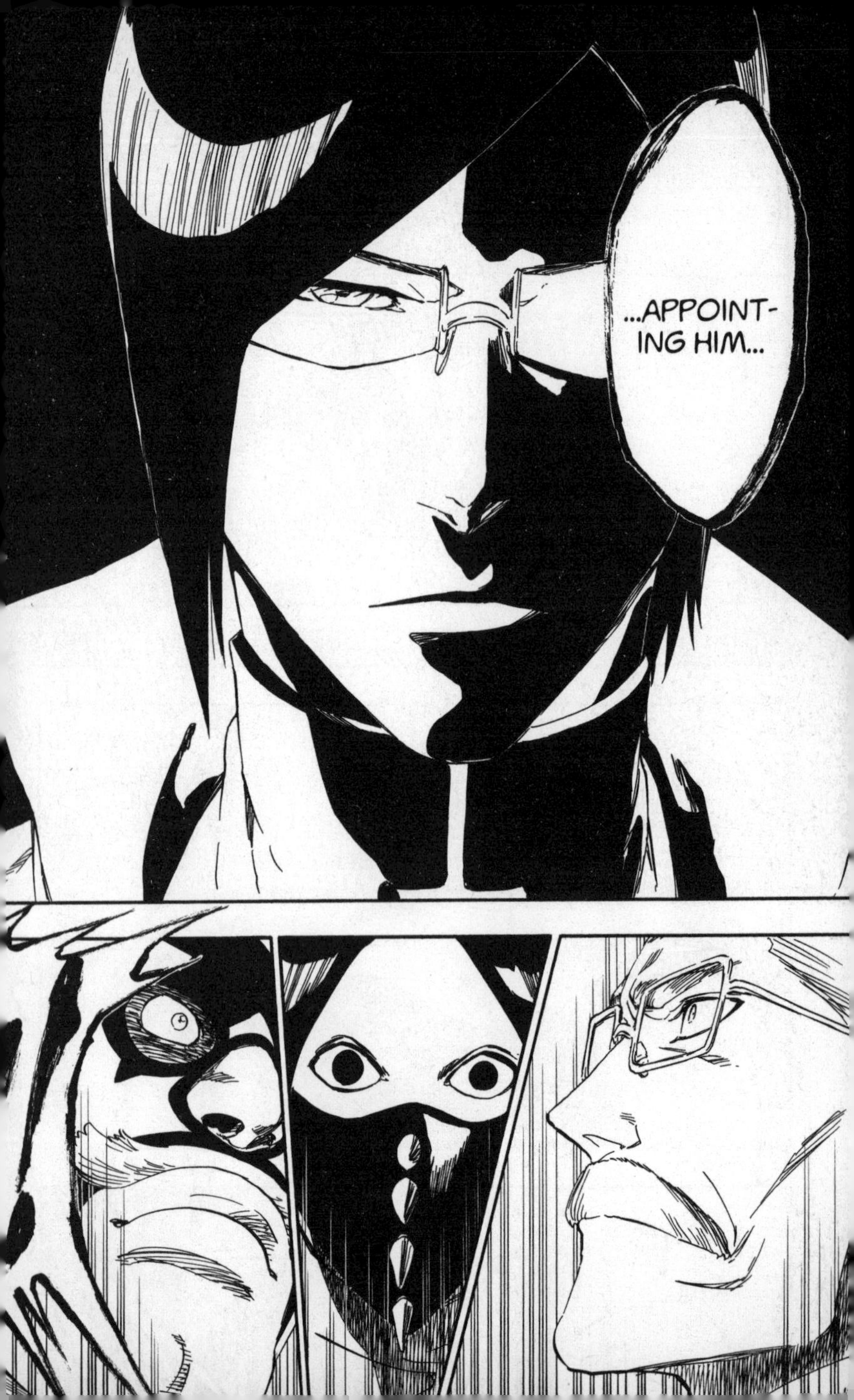
...APPOINT-
ING HIM...

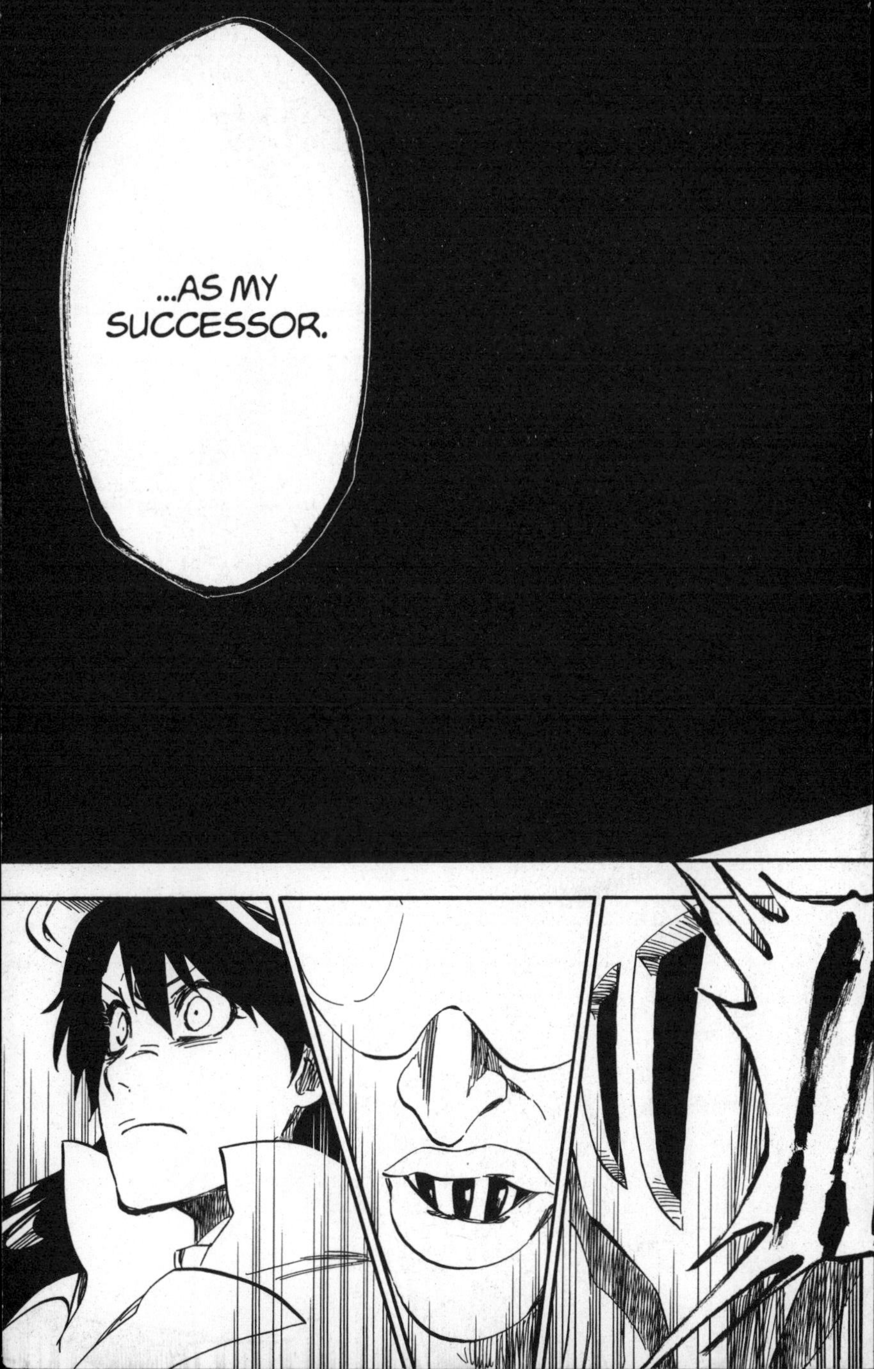
...AS MY SUCCESSOR.

WHAT ...?
WHAT DID HIS MAJESTY JUST SAY ...?
HIS MAJESTY'S SUCCESSOR ...?!
SOME GUY WE DON'T EVEN KNOW ...?!
WHY ...?
ST MP
HOLD ON A SECOND, YOUR MAJESTY !!
!
FWP

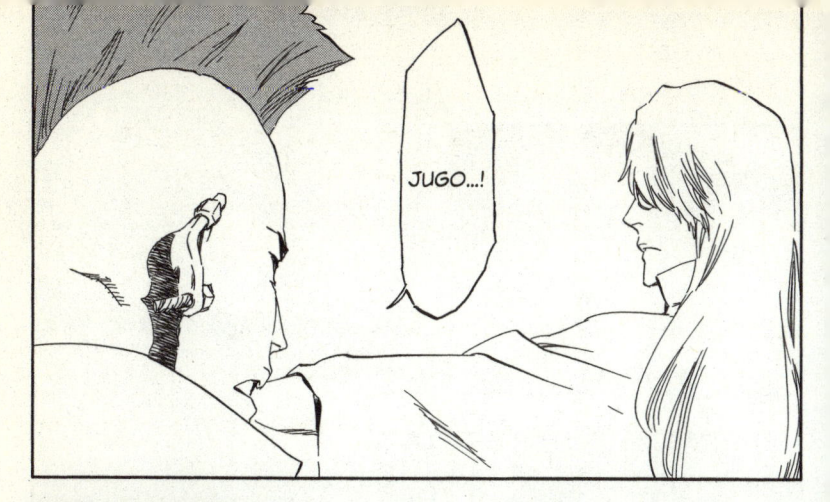

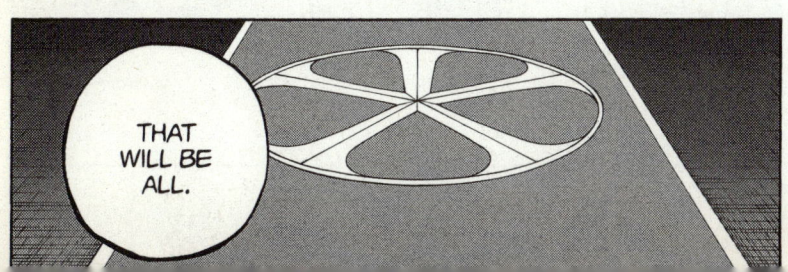

JUGO...!

YOU ALL WILL SOON LEARN FIRSTHAND... NO NEED FOR CONCERN EITHER. I WILL NOT STAND FOR OBJECTIONS.

...HIS POWER IN THE BATTLES TO COME.

THAT WILL BE ALL.

POP
KRAK
KRAK
WHAT THE HELL WAS THAT?!
WHO IS THAT GUY?!
I DON'T UNDER-STAND IT AT ALL!!
WILL SOME-BODY PLEASE EXPLAIN IT TO ME!!

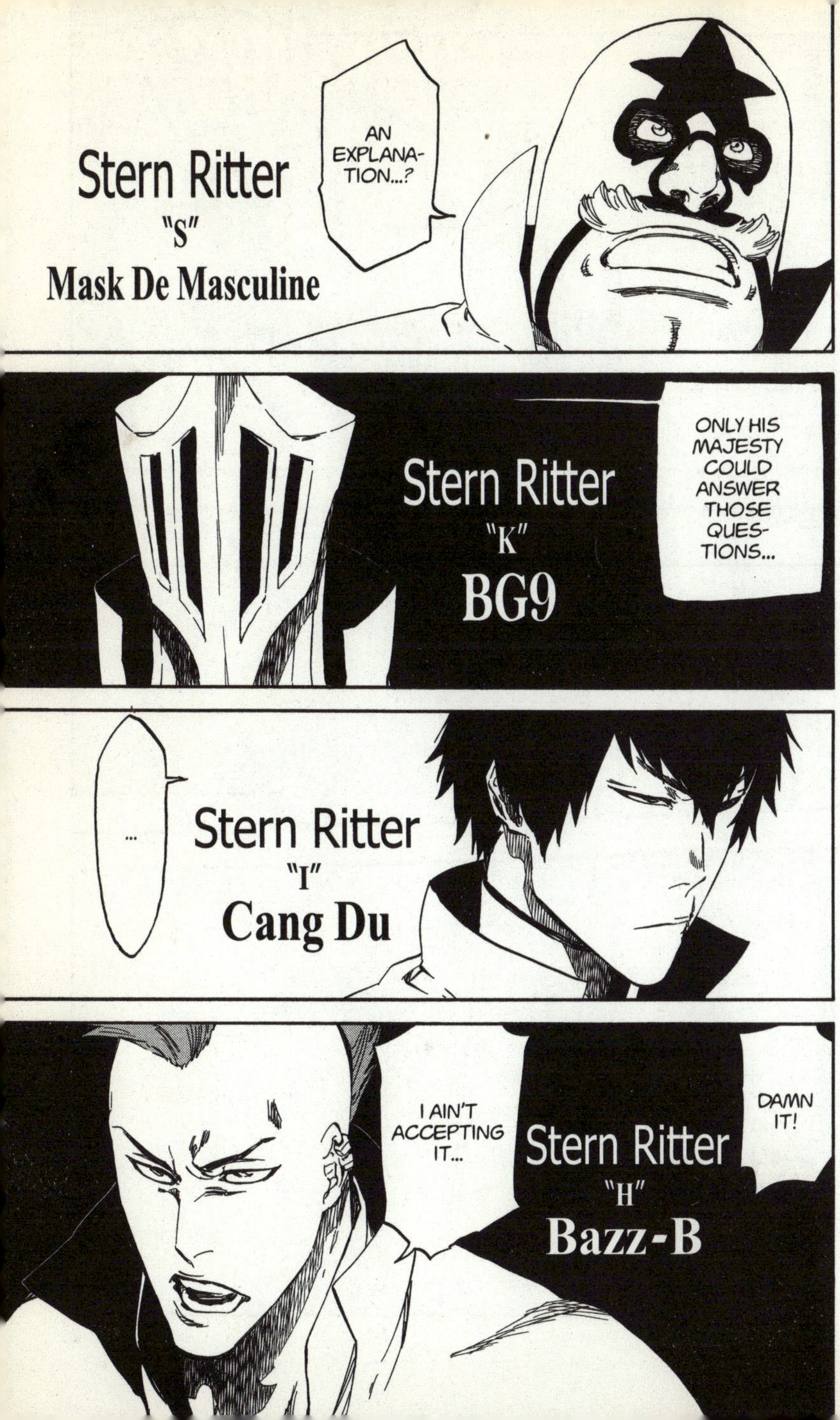
AN EXPLANATION...?
Stern Ritter "S" Mask De Masculine
ONLY HIS MAJESTY COULD ANSWER THOSE QUESTIONS...
Stern Ritter "K" BG9
Stern Ritter "I" Cang Du
...
DAMN IT!
Stern Ritter "H" Bazz-B
I AIN'T ACCEPTING IT...

KRSH
GET OUTTA MY WAY!
I SAID NOT NOW!
SHOOP
H- HEY!
WHERE YOU GOING, BAZZ-B?!
TO HIS MAJESTY'S!
I'M GONNA GO TALK TO HIM!
WHA...
STOP!
YOU THINK HIS MAJESTY WILL TOLERATE THAT?!
BAZZ-B!!
TMP
!

READ THIS WAY

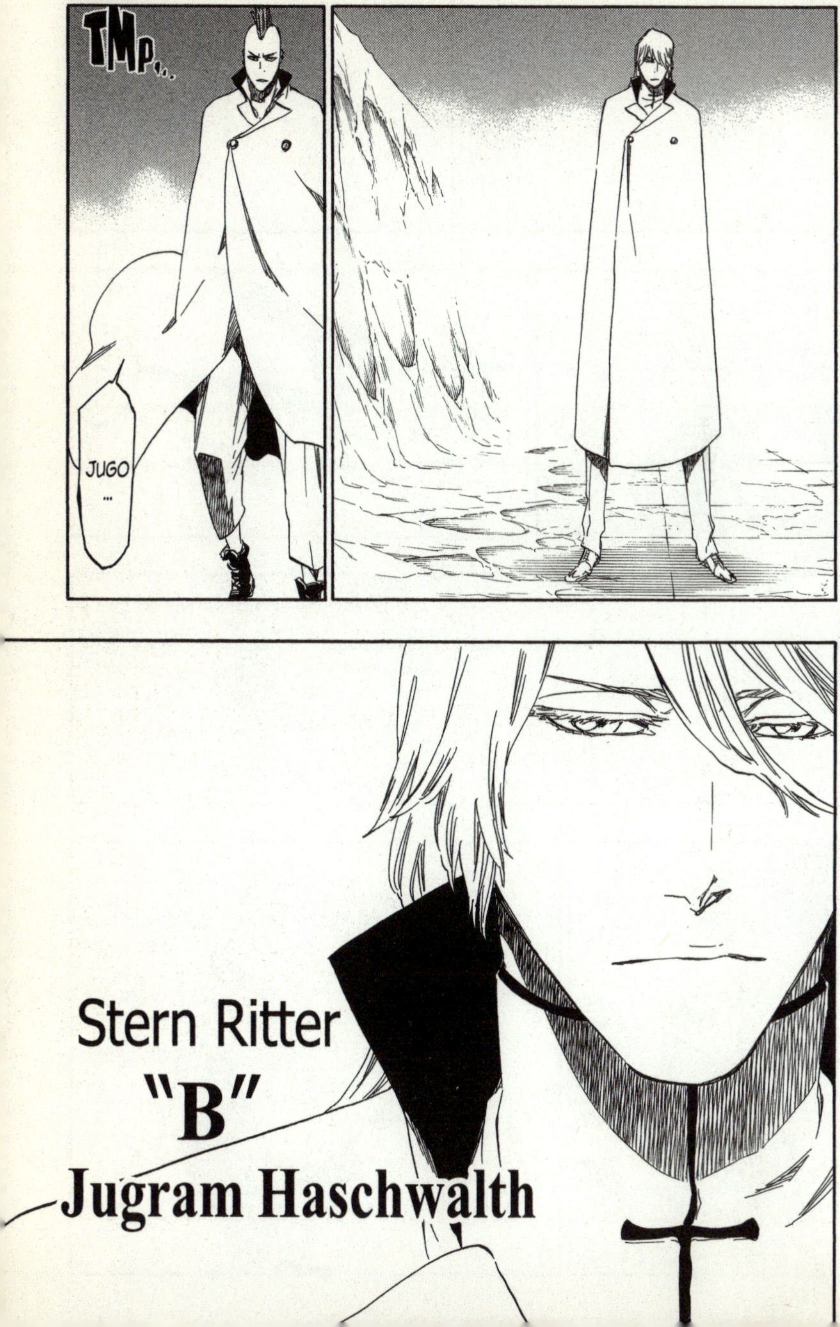
TMP...
JUGO...
Stern Ritter
"B"
Jugram Haschwalth

"WHAT ABOUT YOU? SHOULDN'T YOU BE GOING SOMEWHERE TOO?"

"WHERE ARE YOU GOING, BAZZ-B...?"

"YOU KNOW..."

"I WAS UNDER THE IMPRESSION THAT YOU WERE HIS MAJESTY'S SUCCESSOR."

"MOST OF THE RITTERS WOULD HAVE NO COMPLAINTS IF YOU WERE THE CHOICE."

"AND YET YOU HAVE NO PROBLEM WITH THIS?!"

"TCH... YOU'VE BECOME A COWARD."

"THERE IS NO ROOM FOR ME TO QUESTION IT."

"HIS MAJESTY HAS MADE HIS DECISION."

"WHAT A LETDOWN."

TMP...

THEN GIVE UP YOUR SEAT RIGHT NOW!!
IF YOU'RE JUST GONNA GIVE IT UP TO THAT NOBODY ...
...I'LL TAKE IT FROM YOU!!
CALM DOWN, BAZZ-B.
HUH?!
I AM CALM!
A LOT MORE THAN YOU ARE RIGHT NOW!!

!!

YOU'RE RIGHT...

YOU ARE CALM.

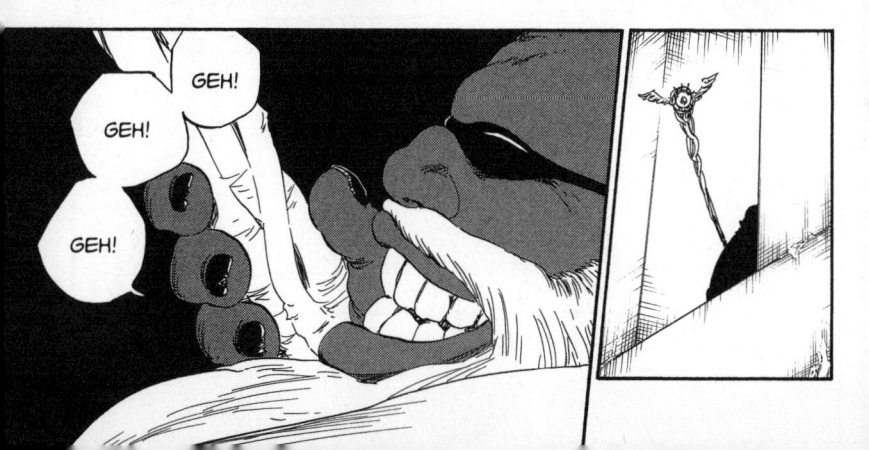

NAKK LE VAAR... WHAT DO YOU THINK YOU'RE DOING...?

YOU DIDN'T CHARGE HEAD-FIRST.

YOU'RE CALM.

VERY CALM...

HELPING YOU. FIGHTING IS NO GOOD.

HIS MAJESTY DOESN'T LIKE CONFLICT AND...

...YOU HAVE EYES ON YOU.

CLAP CLAP CLAP...

Stern Ritter
"D"
Askin Nakk Le Vaar

GEH! GEH! GEH!

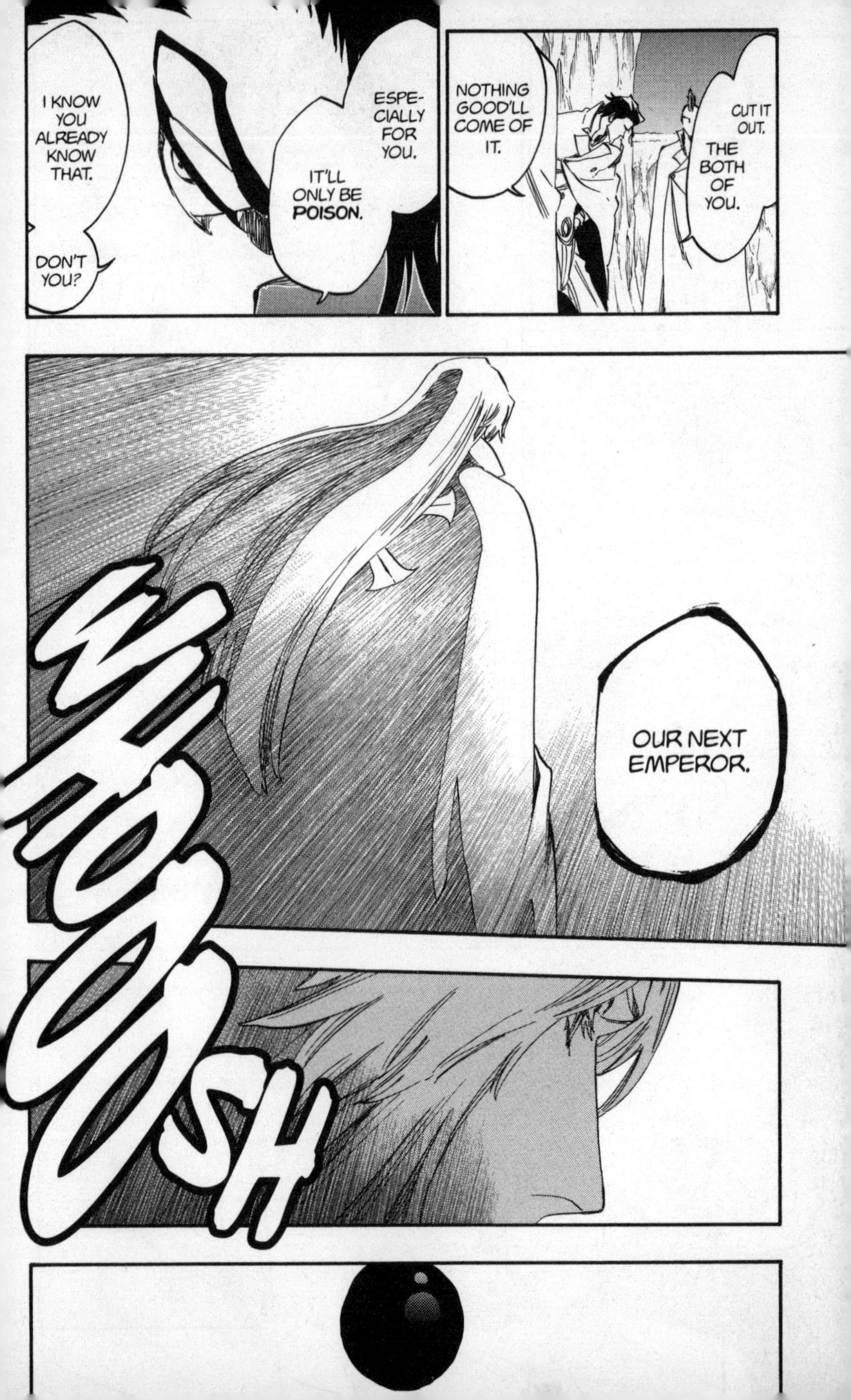
CUT IT OUT. THE BOTH OF YOU.
NOTHING GOOD'LL COME OF IT.
ESPE-CIALLY FOR YOU.
IT'LL ONLY BE **POISON.**
I KNOW YOU ALREADY KNOW THAT.
DON'T YOU?
OUR NEXT EMPEROR.
WHOOOSH

THAT...

...COMPLETES THE RITUAL.

YOUR POWER WILL AWAKEN SOON.

I WILL BESTOW UPON YOU A SCHRIFT. (SACRED LETTER)

YOU SHALL RECEIVE...

...THE SAME LETTER "A" AS ME.

A

WHY...

...AM I THE SUCCESSOR?

...WILL ONLY CREATE FRICTION AMONG YOUR KNIGHTS.

NAMING ME THE SUCCESSOR THE WAY YOU DID...

YOU QUESTION MY DECISION?

544. WALKING WITH WATCHERS

I'M RELIEVED YOU'RE NOT SOME FOOL WHO ACCEPTS THINGS BLINDLY.
BUT YOU MUST THINK HARDER.
IF YOU TAKE A SECOND, IT'S EASY...
...TO UNDERSTAND MY CHOICE.
...
STILL CAN'T FIGURE IT OUT?
THEN LET ME ASK YOU.
URYU.
WHY ARE YOU...
...STILL ALIVE?

!
IT SEEMS YOU PICK THINGS UP QUICKLY.
NINE YEARS AGO ...
...EVERY GEMISCHTE (MIXED-BLOOD) QUINCY PERISHED UNDER...
...THE AUSWÄHLEN I CONDUCTED.
EXCEPT FOR YOU.
YOU ...
...ARE THE ONLY QUINCY EVER TO SURVIVE THE CONSE-CRATION .
THAT IS WHY I...
...REFERRED TO YOU AS THE LAST SURVIVOR.

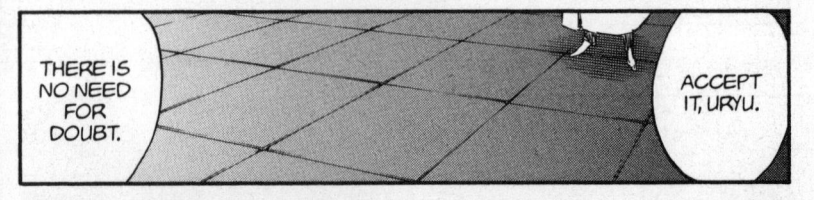

YOU...

...HAVE SOME KIND OF POWER THAT EXCEEDS MY OWN.

THAT IS...

...THE REASON WHY YOU ARE THE SUCCESSOR.

ACCEPT IT, URYU.

THERE IS NO NEED FOR DOUBT.

COME WITH ME.

YES...

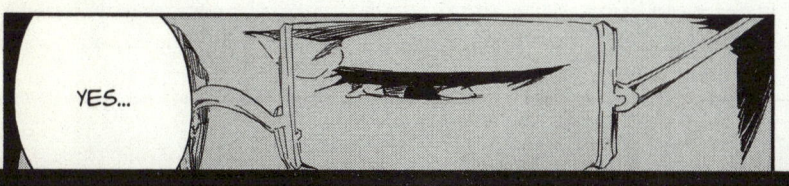

I UNDER-
STAND...

...YOUR
MAJESTY...

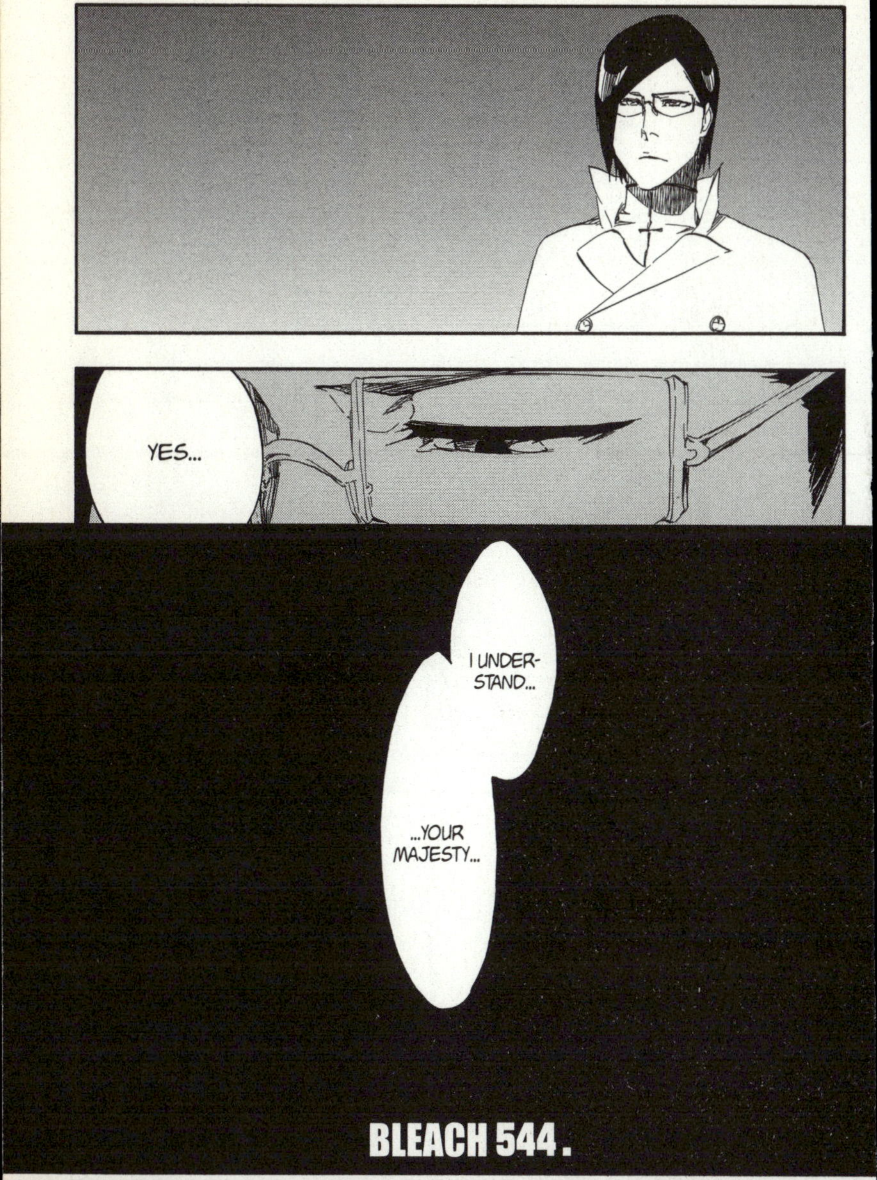

BLEACH 544.

Walking   With   Watchers

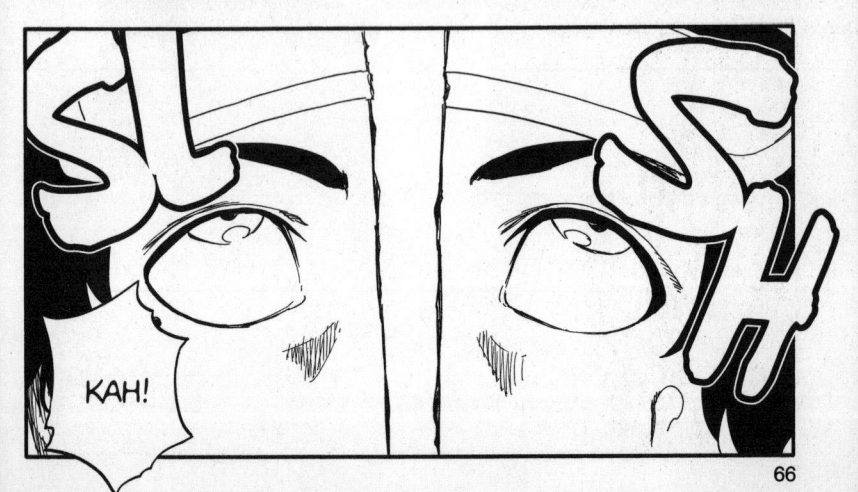

YES, MA'AM!

IT--

IT'S AN HONOR!!

RIGHT THIS SEC-OND!

COME TO MY ROOM. I NEED RELIEF.

FWUSH

M-ME?!

YUP. YOU!

SLSH

KAH!

PLOP PLOP PLOP

PAAAAA...

SPLAAAT

LOOK AT THE MESS YOU MADE AGAIN!!

AW, C'MON.

KCHK

TMP TMP TMP

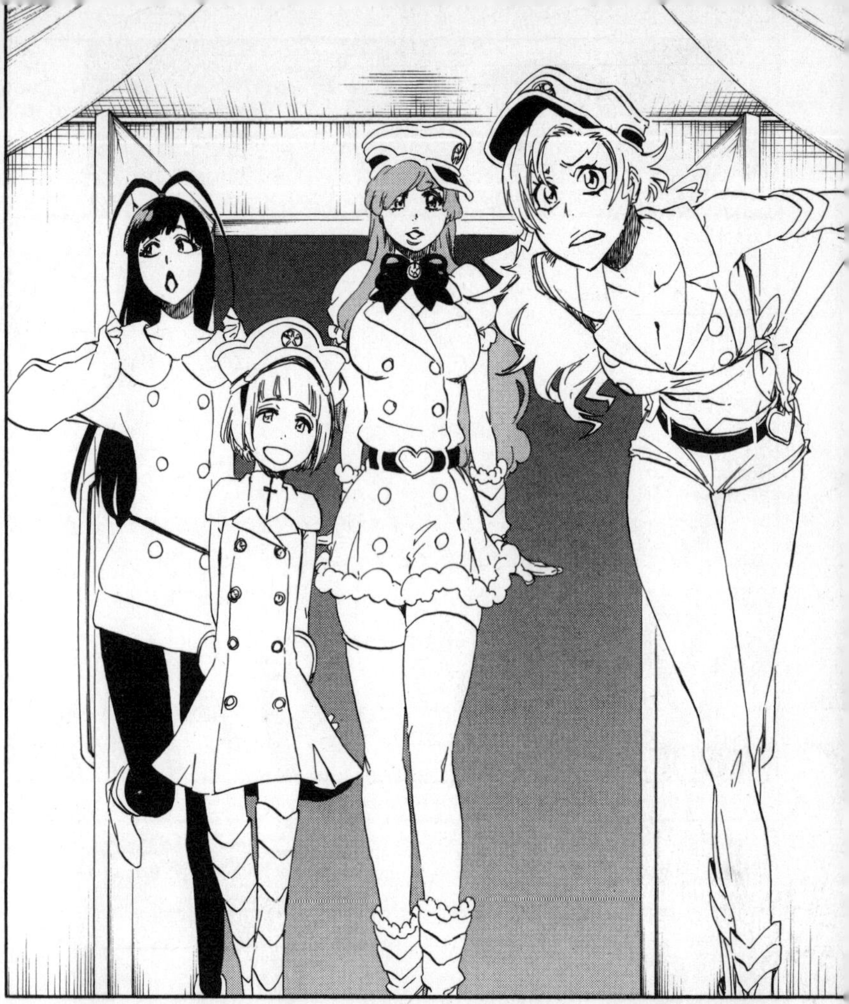

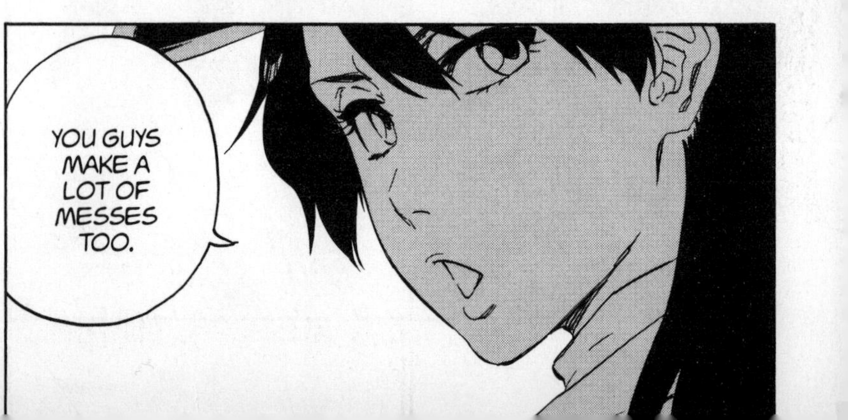
YOU GUYS MAKE A LOT OF MESSES TOO.

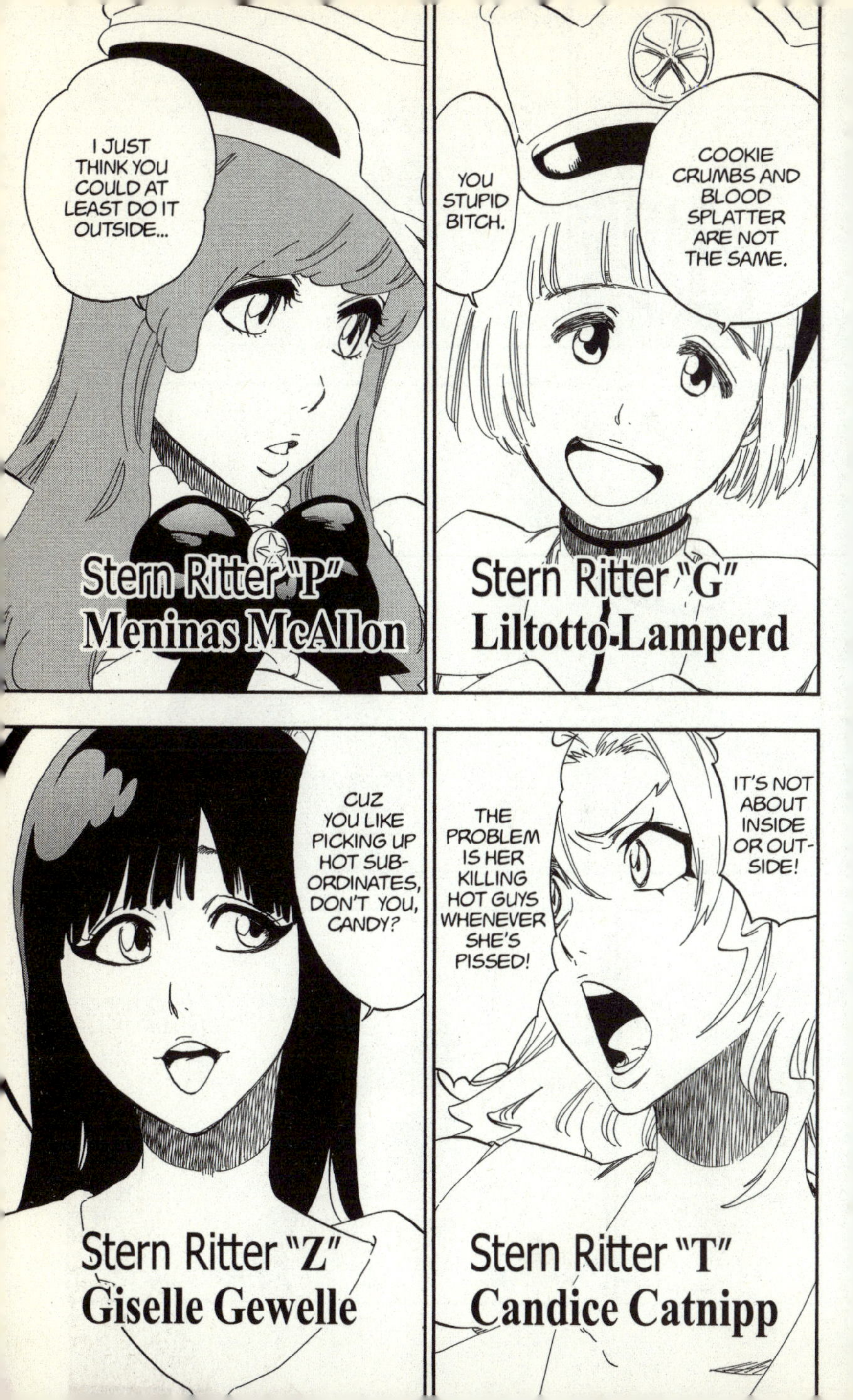
COOKIE CRUMBS AND BLOOD SPLATTER ARE NOT THE SAME.
YOU STUPID BITCH.
Stern Ritter "G"
Liltotto Lamperd
I JUST THINK YOU COULD AT LEAST DO IT OUTSIDE...
Stern Ritter "P"
Meninas McAllon
IT'S NOT ABOUT INSIDE OR OUT-SIDE!
THE PROBLEM IS HER KILLING HOT GUYS WHENEVER SHE'S PISSED!
Stern Ritter "T"
Candice Catnipp
CUZ YOU LIKE PICKING UP HOT SUB-ORDINATES, DON'T YOU, CANDY?
Stern Ritter "Z"
Giselle Gewelle

HUH ?!
THAT'S NOT WHAT I'M SAYING!
YOU PICKING A FIGHT WITH ME, GIGI?!
LOOK AT ME !!
GLUNK
YOU MIND KEEPING IT DOWN...?
I GOT A LOT ON MY MIND RIGHT NOW.
K...R E... E...
WHAT ...?
WHAT'S BOTHERING YOU?

READ THIS WAY

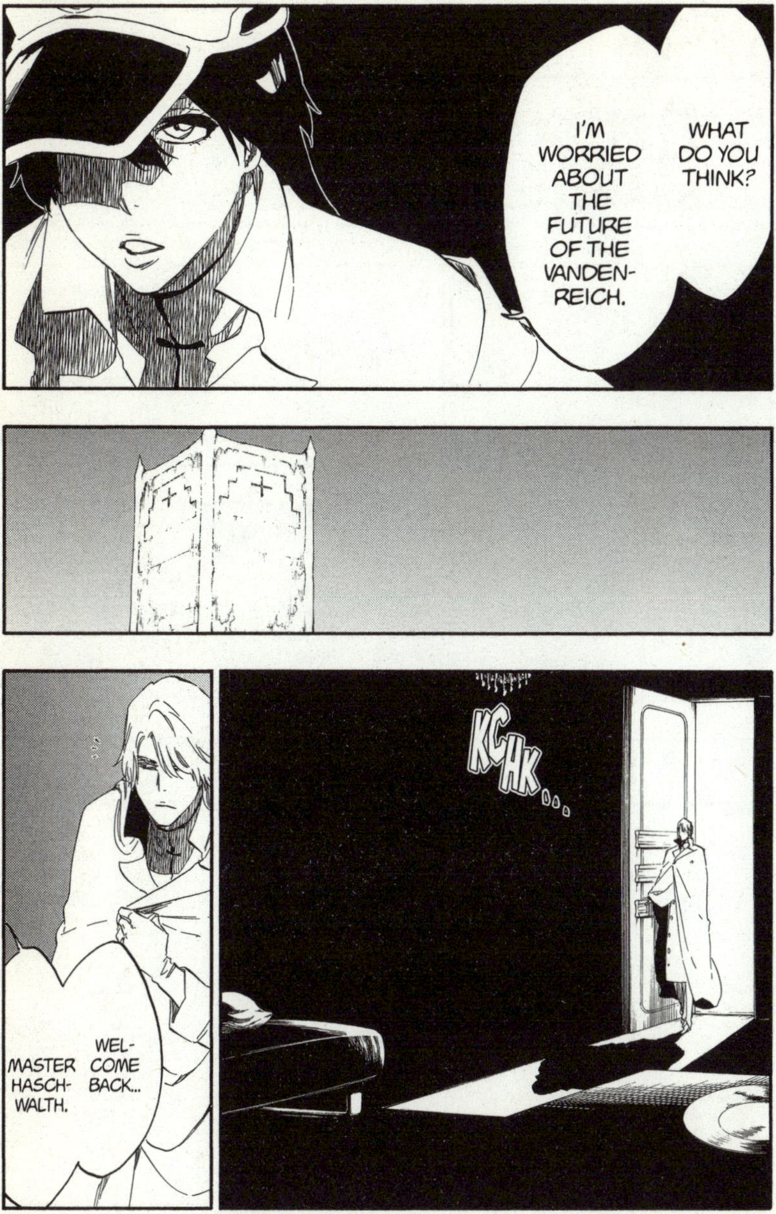

"YOU'RE STILL UP?"

"IT'S LATE."

"GET SOME REST."

"I HEARD ABOUT IT. HIS MAJESTY'S ANNOUNCEMENT."

"YOU DON'T APPROVE?"

"YOU CAN'T UNDERSTAND IT?"

"DO YOU, MASTER HASCHWALTH?"

"IT MAY NOT BE MY PLACE TO SAY."

"BUT I..."

"...BELIEVE HIS MAJESTY COULD USE YOUR COUNSEL."

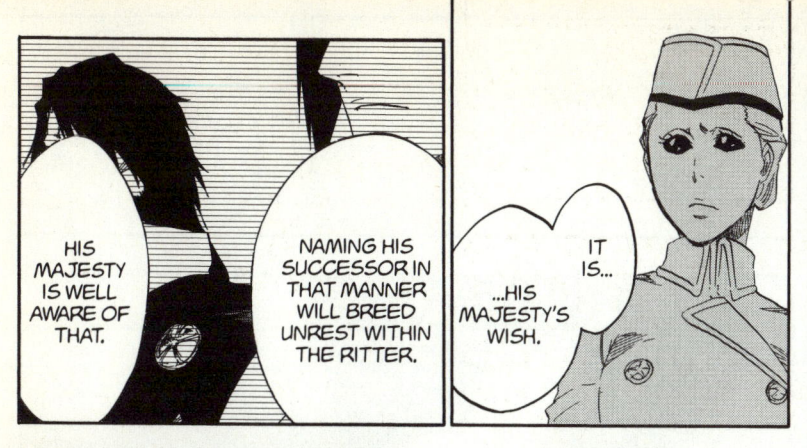

HIS MAJESTY IS WELL AWARE OF THAT.

NAMING HIS SUCCESSOR IN THAT MANNER WILL BREED UNREST WITHIN THE RITTER.

IT IS...

...HIS MAJESTY'S WISH.

THEN THERE IS ONLY ONE ANSWER.

IT WAS...

...HIS MAJESTY'S INTENTION TO CAUSE UNREST.

NO MATTER WHO HE IS...

NO MATTER WHAT KIND OF POWER HE POSSESSES...

NO MATTER WHAT HE'S UP TO...

HE NOW...

...WILL BE DIRECTED AT URYU ISHIDA.

UNREST CAUSES SCRUTINY IN THE RANKS.

MORE SO...

...ALL OF THAT SCRUTINY...

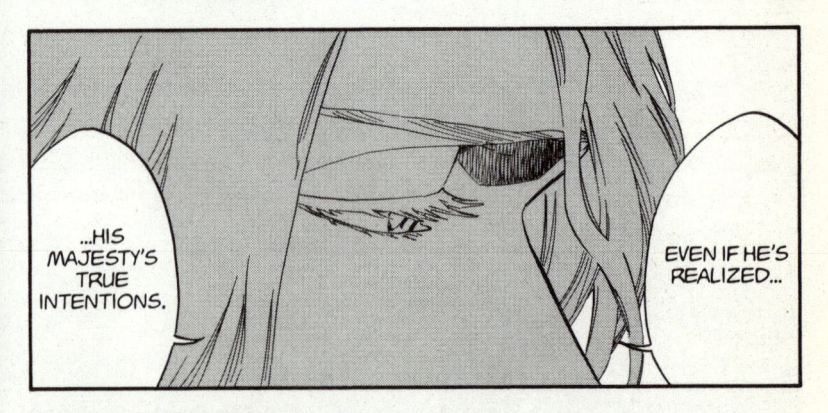

...CANNOT MAKE THE SLIGHTEST MOVE.

HIS ONLY...

...PATH NOW IS TO DEDICATE HIMSELF...

...TO HIS MAJESTY'S WILL.

EVEN IF HE'S REALIZED...

...HIS MAJESTY'S TRUE INTENTIONS.

FLOP

I'M FINALLY HERE!!

PHAAA!

THUD

RUSTL RUSTL

I KNOW TRAVELING'S A PART OF TRAINING, BUT THIS NEGAL RUIN WAS SO FAR AWAY...

YUCK... WHAT IS THIS...?

WHAT'S IT MADE FROM ANYWAYS...? I'M SCARED...

WONDER HOW CHAD IS DOING...

KRSH

CHU CHEW CHEW

YOU MUST BE TIRED TOO, PERO!

HE WAS SO CONCERNED WITH WHAT THIS DELICIOUS POTATO-LIKE THING WAS MADE FROM. I WONDER IF HE GOT HERE ALL RIGHT...?

| HE'S EQUIPPED WITH A CAMERA, SO DON'T WORRY! I'LL BE RIGHT THERE IF ANYTHING HAPPENS! | I'LL HAVE HIM GO WITH YOU JUST TO BE SAFE! | NOT AT ALL PERO! | NO. |

CHAD! GOOD, YOU GOT HERE BEFORE ME...

TOOK YOU LONG ENOUGH, INOUE!

...HE DIDN'T COME WHEN I WAS IN DANGER.

WHY WOULD HE SAY THAT...?

IS WHAT HE SAID, BUT...

RMBL RMBL RMBL

EVERYBODY'S HERE!

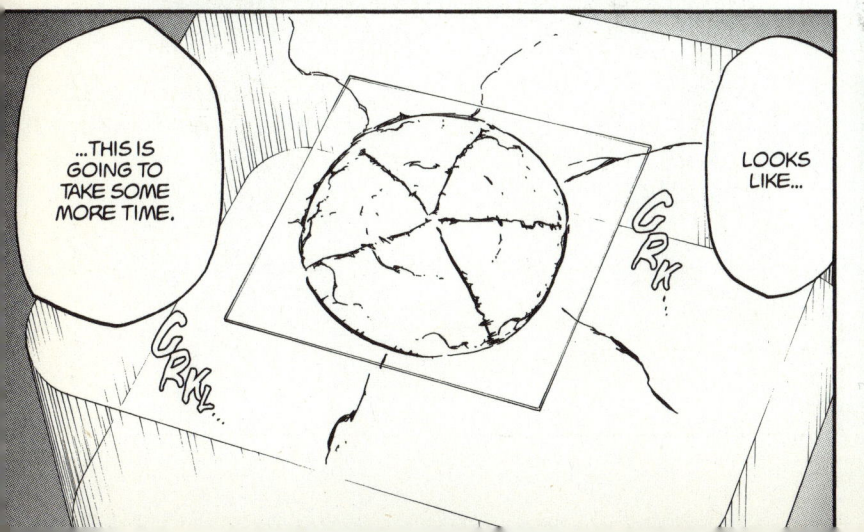

WAIT?

WHAT...?!

EVERYBODY...?

SO SHE GOT HERE SAFELY...

GOOD...

LOOKS LIKE...

...THIS IS GOING TO TAKE SOME MORE TIME.

GRK...
GRK...

KUROSAKI CLINIC

TINK TINK TINK TINK

SHAAAA

TIME TO EAT!

DAD! KARIN!

545. BLUE STRIPES

OKEY-DOKEY! LET ME GET RID OF THIS PATIENT AND I'LL BE RIGHT THERE!!
HEY! ARE YOU TALKING ABOUT ME, DOC?!
HOLD ON!
I'LL BE DOWN AFTER I KILL THIS BOSS!!
NO MORE AFTER THAT, OKAY?!
I KNOW!
I WISH...
...ICHIGO WAS BACK FROM TRAINING CAMP.

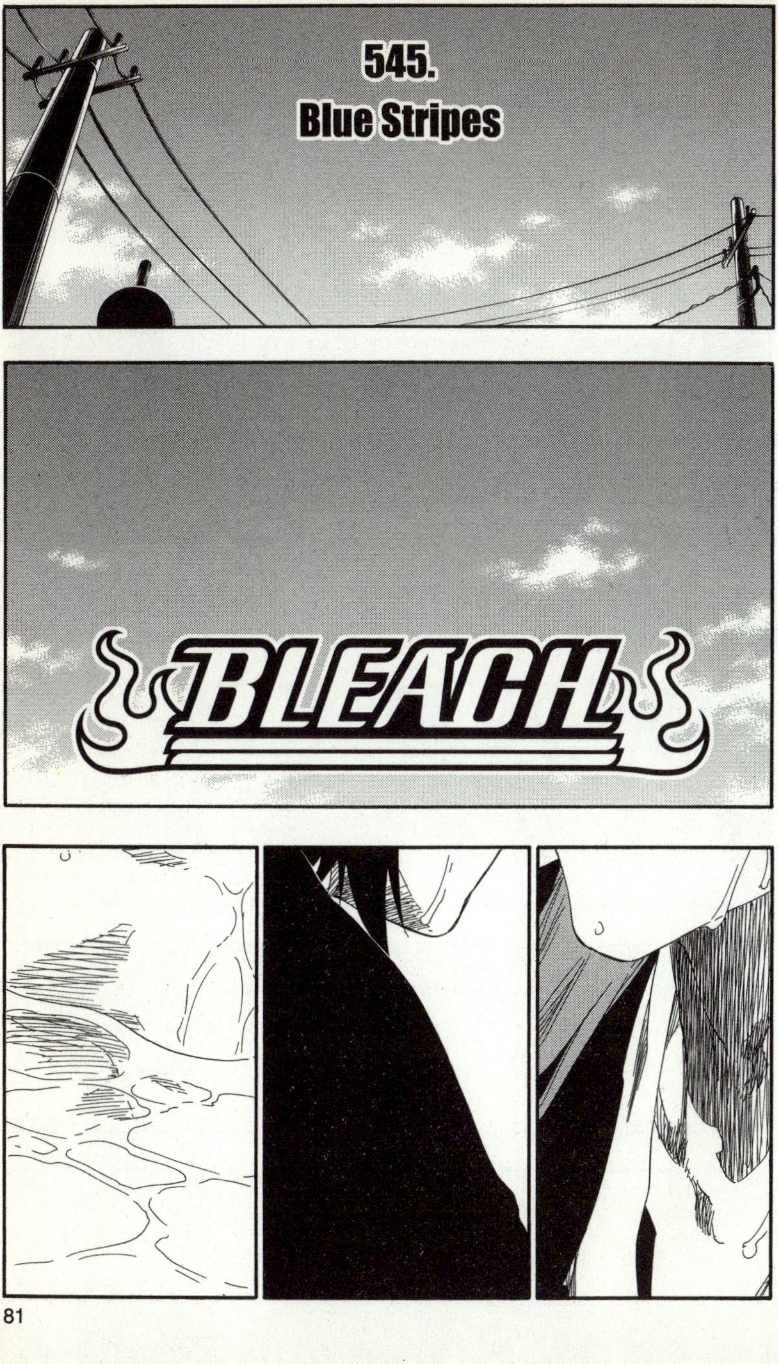
545.
Blue Stripes
BLEACH

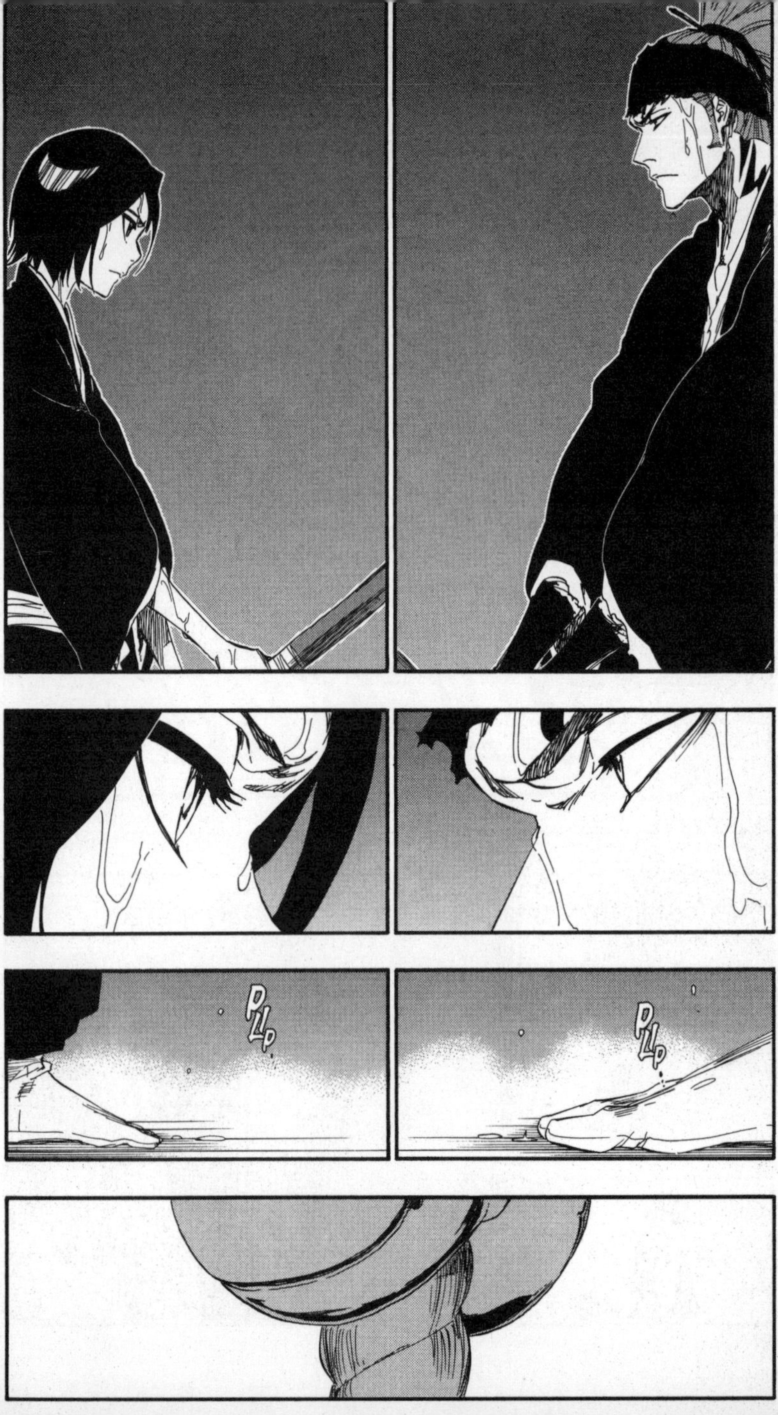
PLIP
PLIP

CLANGCLANG CLANGCLANG
PHAAAAAAAA!!
HUWEE !!
DAMN, THAT'S TOUGH !!
THUD
SHUT UP!
WHAT'S SO TOUGH ABOUT STANDING STILL AND FACING EACH OTHER!
YOU SHUT UP. IT'S NOT FOR ME!
STANDING STILL OR POINTING A SWORD AT A FRIEND!
I-I DON'T LIKE POINTING MY SWORD AT FRIENDS EITHER!
SEE, YOU'RE EX-HAUSTED TOO.

...WE'RE STILL NOT USED TO THE AIR HERE.

PLUS...

THE REISHI DENSITY OF THE ATMOSPHERE HERE IS INCREDIBLE.

TRUE.

BEEP BEEP BEEP

I HAVE NO IDEA WHAT EFFECT THIS KIND OF REISHI DENSITY HAS ON US...

IT DOESN'T FEEL COMPLETELY OVERWHELMING NOW...

BUT IT STILL FEELS LIKE BEING UNDERWATER.

READ THIS WAY
YES, THIS IS KUCHIKI!
YES...
REALLY?!
YES!
YES!
?
WHO IS IT?
THAT WAS KIRINJI!
OH.
WHAT'S UP WITH NOT SHOWING MY FACE IN A FLASHBACK?
THE GREASER FROM THE HOT SPRING.
WHEN DID YOU GUYS EXCHANGE NUMBERS...?
MY BROTHER'S...
...HEALED!
THAT WAS A LONG BATH...
麒麟殿
YOU'RE THE FIRST TO BATHE THIS LONG IN MY HOT SPRING.
WELL?
YOU LIGHT-HEADED AT ALL?
NO NEED FOR YOU TO WORRY...

I'M AWARE...

...THAT MY POWER IS STILL NOT DEVELOPED ENOUGH FOR ME TO GET LIGHT-HEADED.

...I NOW NEED TO GAIN A POWER DESERVING OF FEELING LIGHT-HEADED.

HAVING SURVIVED...

YUP, THEN GO THERE...

WAIT, THAT MEANS HE'LL EAT, TRAIN HIS SWORD, THEN...

HE'S HEALED?!

GREAT!

THAT PLACE WAS AWFUL...
A MEASUREMENT FROM HELL...
YEAH...
STRIPPED NAKED...
I DON'T EVEN WANT TO THINK ABOUT IT...
HEY!
REN-JI!
WHY ARE YOU TRYING TO REMEMBER IT?!
NO! DON'T DO IT!
REN-JI!!
HUH?

DO NOT RESPOND WITH A QUESTION.
YOU HEARD WHAT I SAID.
I SAID TAKE OFF YOUR LOINCLOTH TOO.
WAIT, WAIT. WE'RE TAKING MEASUREMENTS FOR A SHIHAKUSHO, RIGHT?
WHY CAN'T WE DO THAT WITH MY LOINCLOTH ON?
I SEE...
ALL RIGHT.
I UNDERSTAND.
I'LL TAKE MEASUREMENTS AFTER I REMOVE YOUR JEWELS.
OKAY! I'M TAKING IT OFF RIGHT NOW!!!
HMMM...
GASP
YOU BACK, RENJI?!
GOOD!
I'M GLAD YOU DIDN'T REACH THE PART WHERE YOU TOOK IT OFF!!
BUT...
...MORE IMPORTANTLY, TO THINK MY BROTHER HAS TO GO THROUGH THE SAME HUMILIATION...
POOR BYAKUYA...
MORE IMPORTANTLY...?

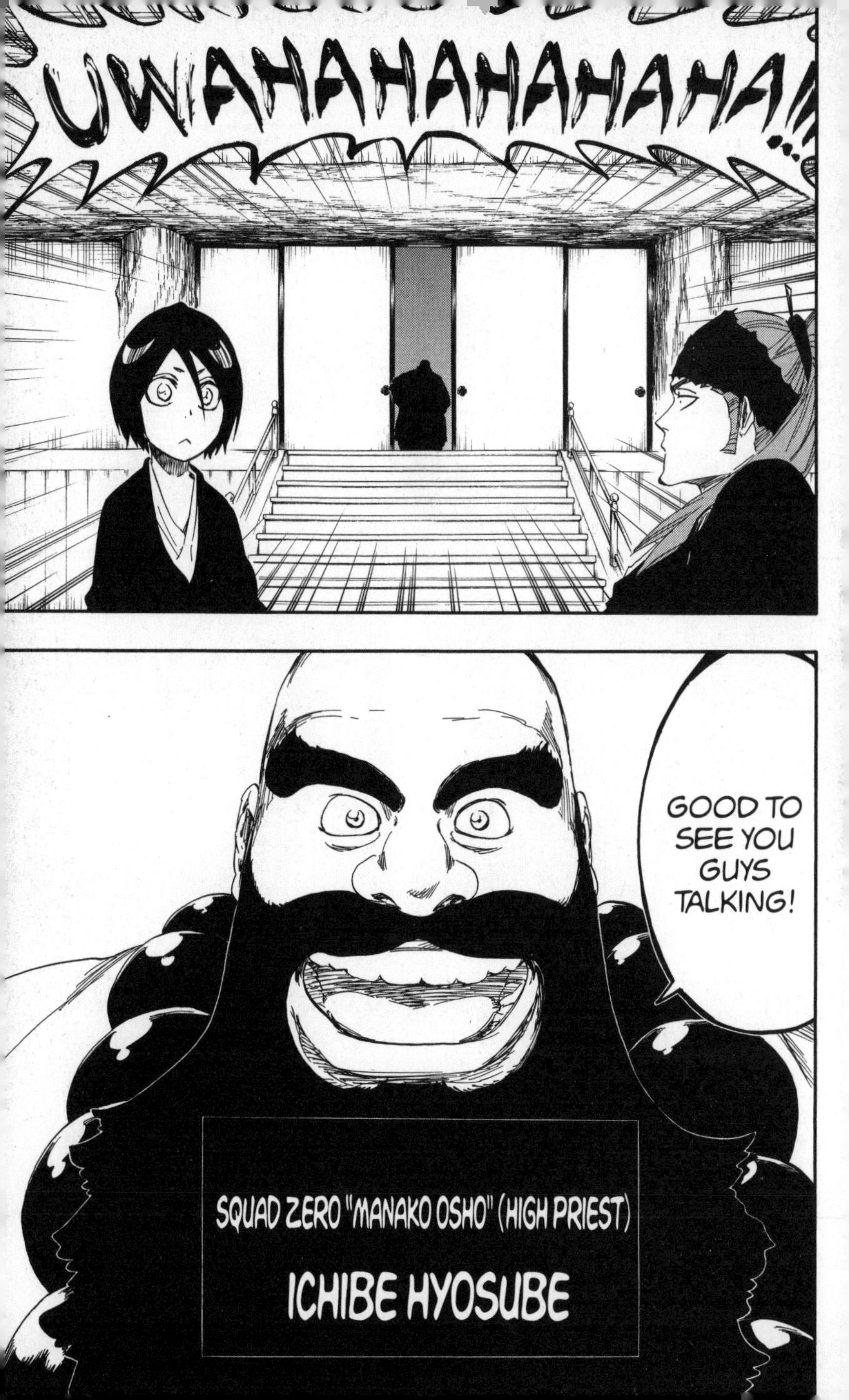
UWAHAHAHAHAHAHA!!...!!
GOOD TO SEE YOU GUYS TALKING!
SQUAD ZERO "MANAKO OSHO" (HIGH PRIEST)
ICHIBE HYOSUBE

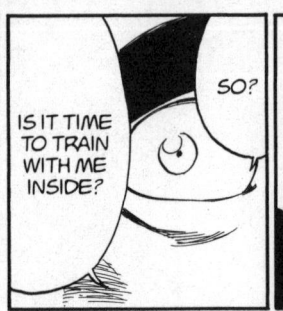

IS IT TIME TO TRAIN WITH ME INSIDE?	SO?	THIS IS QUITE AN IMPROVEMENT. WELL DONE! WHEN YOU FIRST GOT HERE, THE REISHI WAS SO THICK YOU TWO COULD BARELY MOVE OR BREATHE.

FWP

YES, SIR!!!

LIKE I SAID!

"I CAN TELL EVEN OVER THE PHONE THAT YOU'RE NOT BOWING YOUR HEAD!!!"

"HEAD DOWN? YEAH RIGHT!!"

"I'M BEGGING FOR YOUR HELP, WITH MY HEAD DOWN!!"

"THIS ISN'T AN ORDER!!"

"THAT WAS FAST!!"

"THERE'S A PACKAGE FROM THE SOUL SOCIETY."

"THEY ACTUALLY HAVE A POSTAL SERVICE?!"

"DON'T HANG UP, DAMN IT!!"

"HEY?!"

"HIYORI."

"YOU'RE THE ONLY ONE WHO CAN DO IT!!"

"HOW DO YOU LIKE THAT CHOSEN-ONE FEELING?! PRETTY GOOD, HUH?! LATER!!"

"LOOK, I'M COUNTING ON YOU, OKAY?!"

"IT WAS SENT FROM TWO PEOPLE."

"SHINJI HIRAKO AND..."

"...MAYURI KUROTSUCHI."

AW, DAMN IT! ALL RIGHT, I'LL FREAKIN' DO IT!!!
FIXING THE SUPER PAIN-IN-THE-BUTT DISTORTION BETWEEN THE WORLD OF THE LIVING AND THE SOUL SOCIETY CREW...
...HAS BEEN FORMED!!
FORMED...?
WE'RE A PART OF IT?
OF COURSE!!!
ZSH...
ICHIGO?

READ THIS WAY

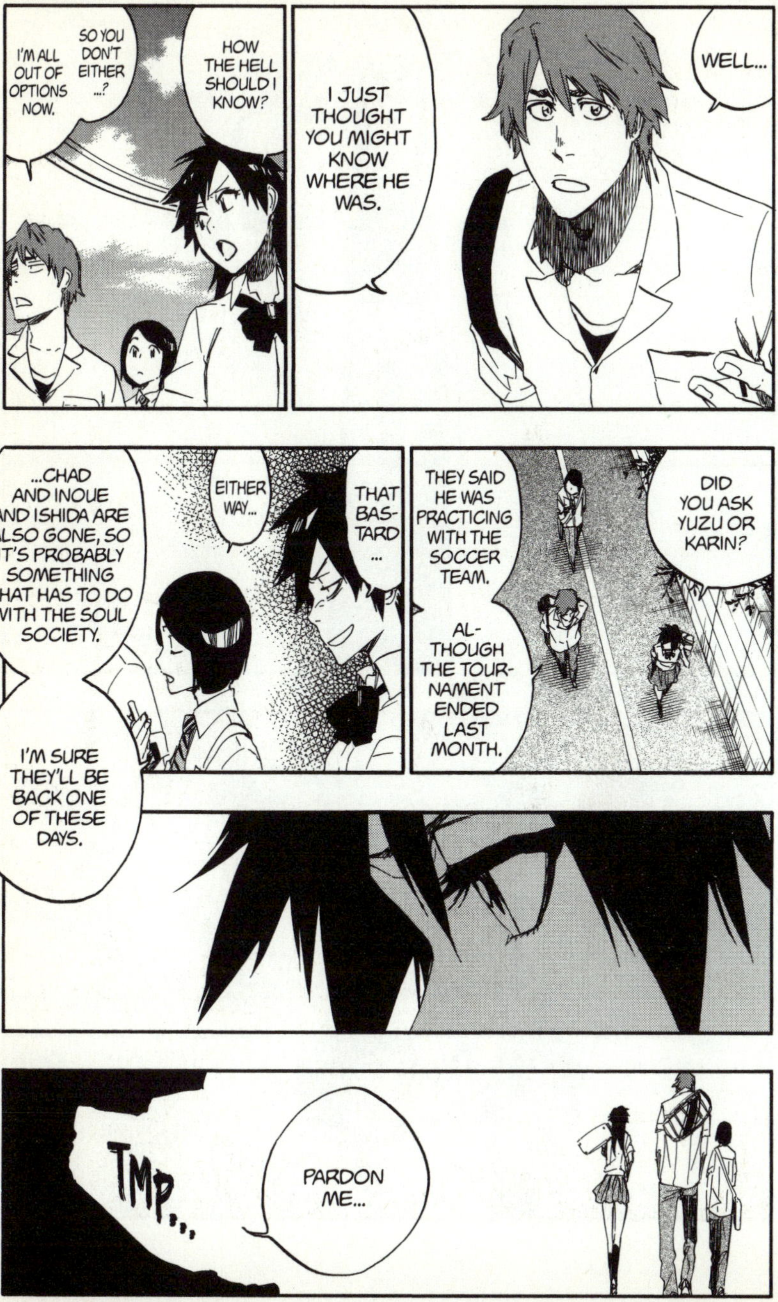

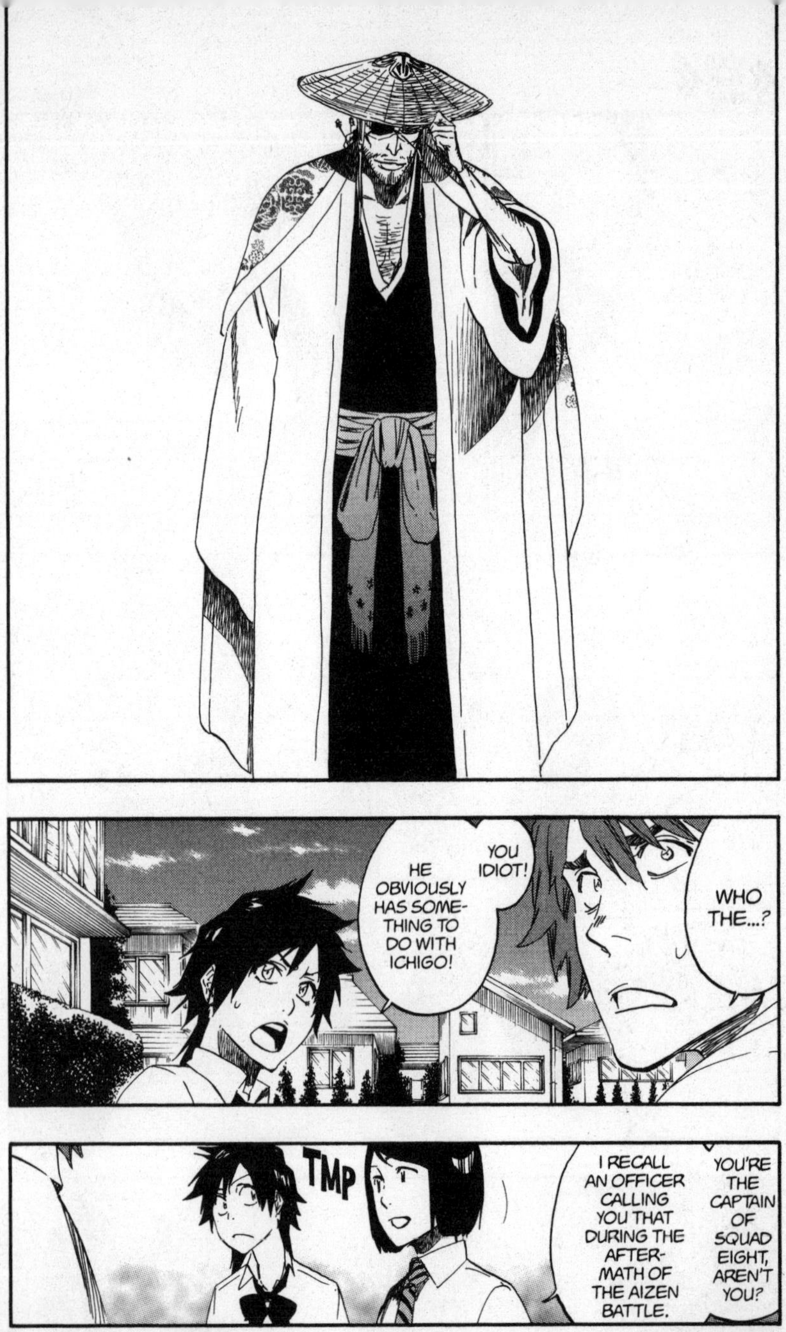
WHO THE...?
YOU IDIOT!
HE OBVIOUSLY HAS SOME-THING TO DO WITH ICHIGO!
YOU'RE THE CAPTAIN OF SQUAD EIGHT, AREN'T YOU?
I RECALL AN OFFICER CALLING YOU THAT DURING THE AFTER-MATH OF THE AIZEN BATTLE.
TMP

READ THIS WAY

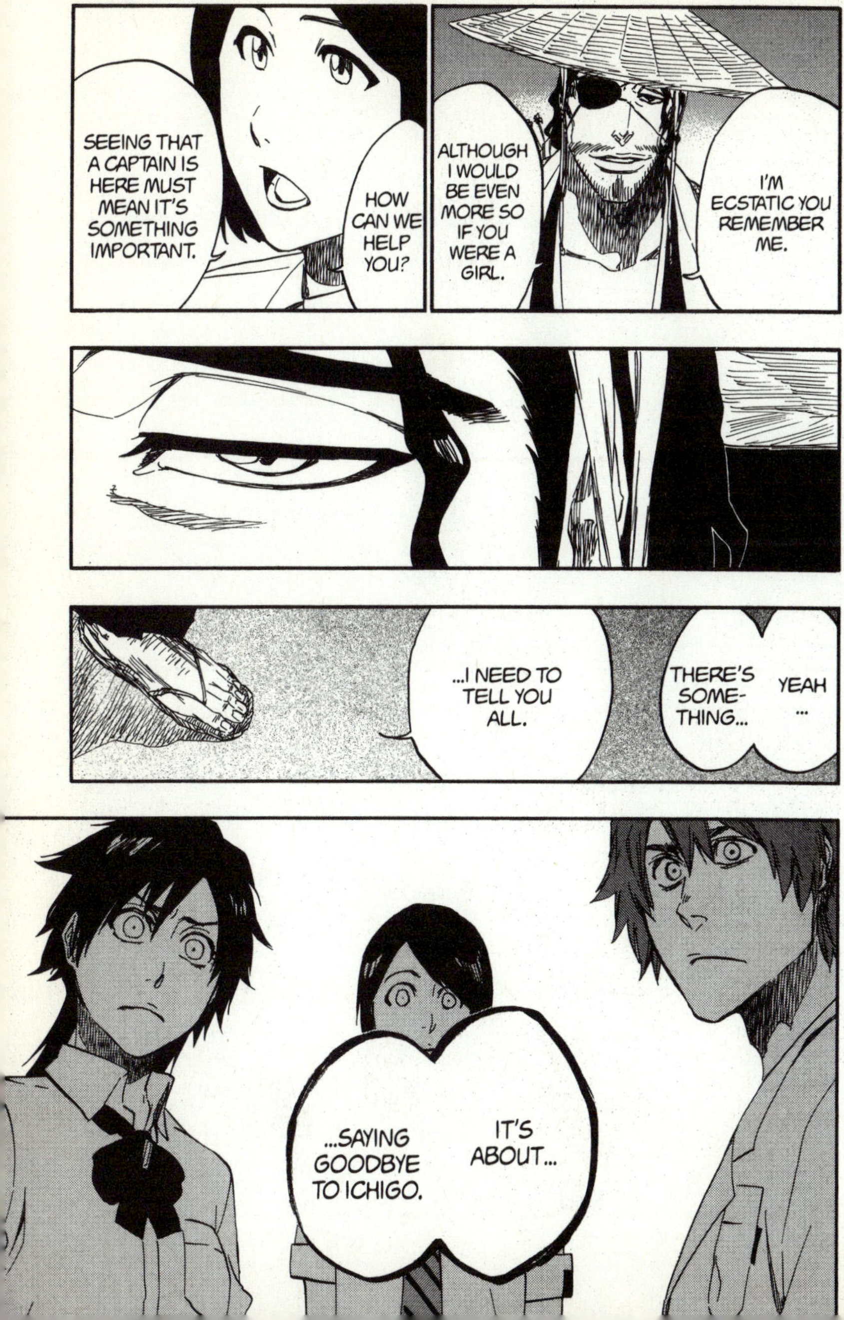

SOCCER PRACTICE, EH...?

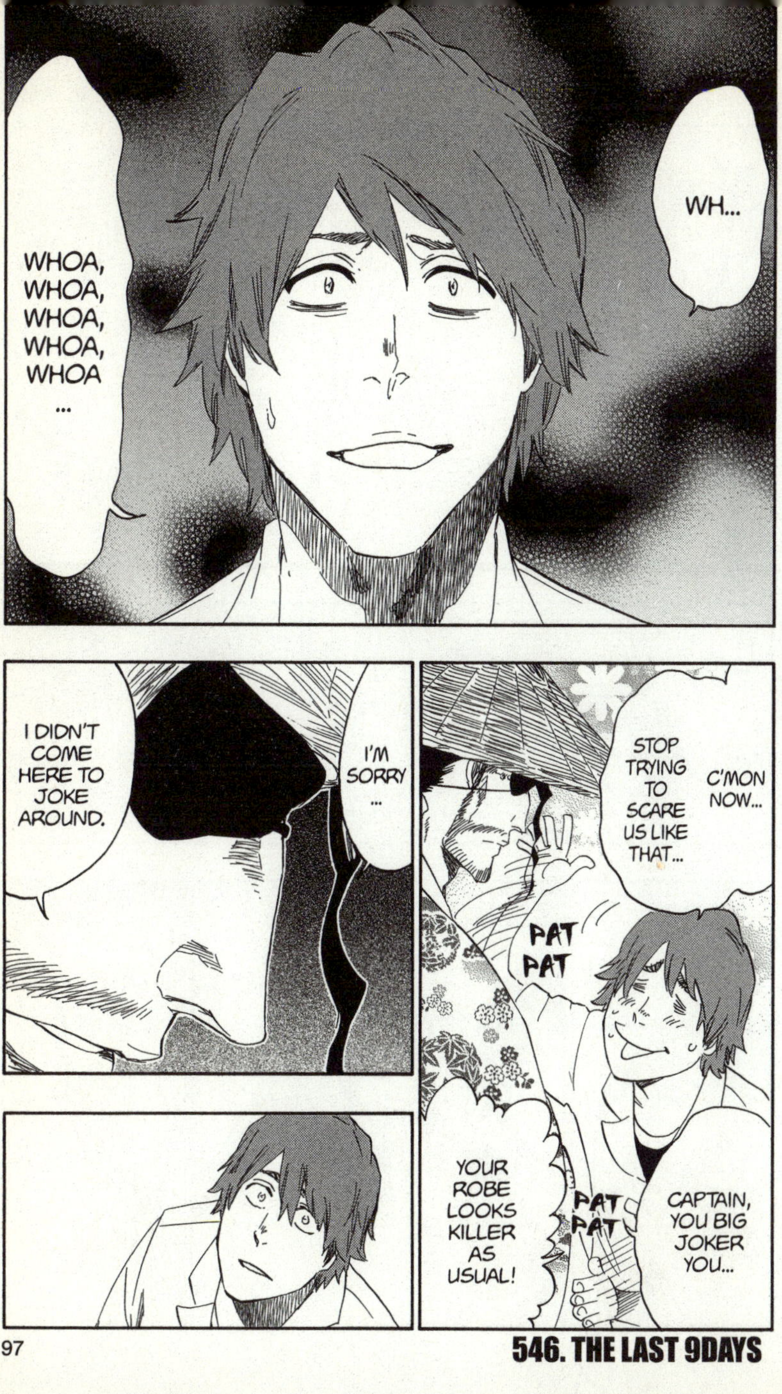
WH...
WHOA, WHOA, WHOA, WHOA, WHOA ...
C'MON NOW...
STOP TRYING TO SCARE US LIKE THAT...
PAT PAT
CAPTAIN, YOU BIG JOKER YOU...
PAT PAT
YOUR ROBE LOOKS KILLER AS USUAL!
I'M SORRY ...
I DIDN'T COME HERE TO JOKE AROUND.

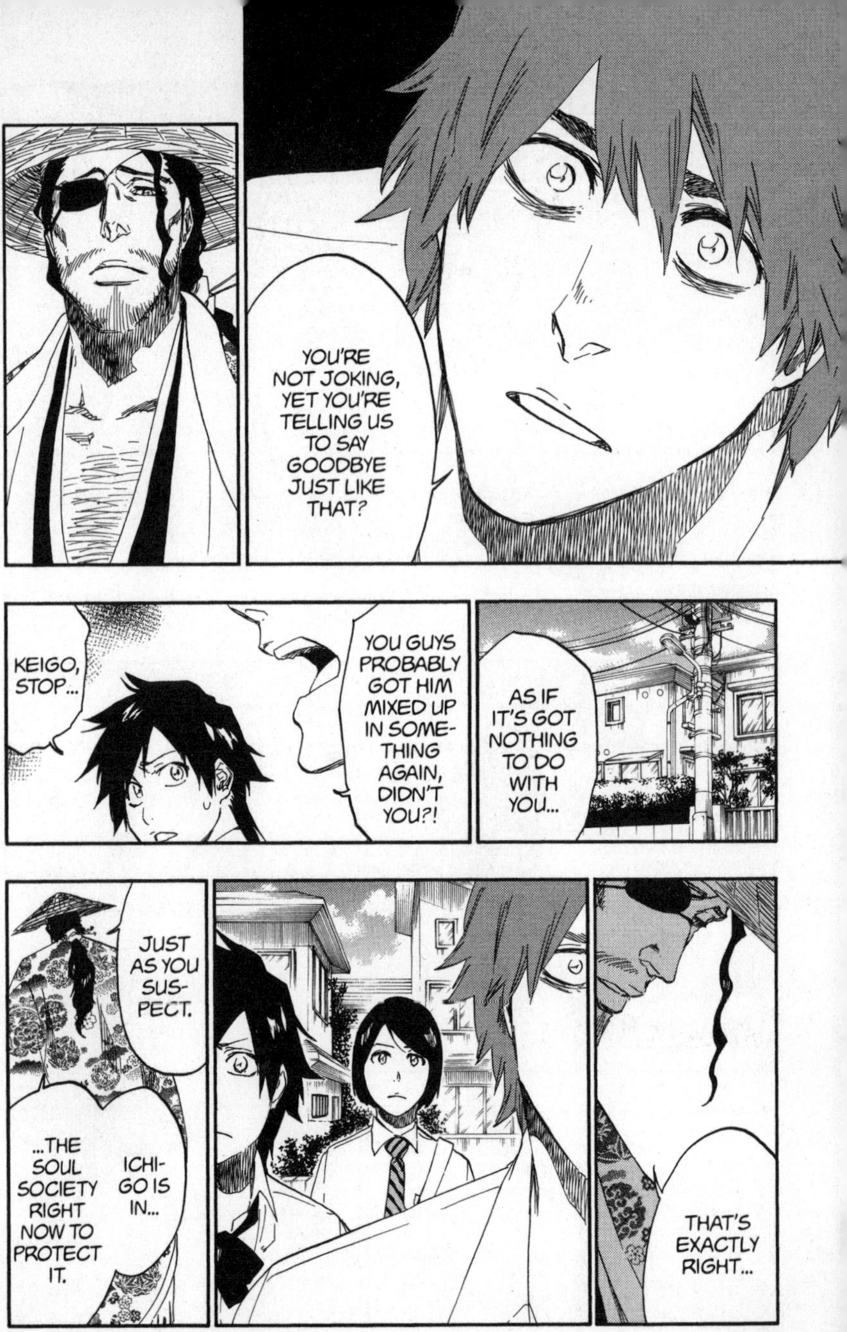
YOU'RE NOT JOKING, YET YOU'RE TELLING US TO SAY GOODBYE JUST LIKE THAT?
AS IF IT'S GOT NOTHING TO DO WITH YOU...
YOU GUYS PROBABLY GOT HIM MIXED UP IN SOME-THING AGAIN, DIDN'T YOU?!
KEIGO, STOP...
THAT'S EXACTLY RIGHT...
JUST AS YOU SUS-PECT.
ICHI-GO IS IN...
...THE SOUL SOCIETY RIGHT NOW TO PROTECT IT.

THAT'S FINE...
THAT'S WHO HE IS.
THAT'S WHY WE'RE FRIENDS WITH HIM.
BUT...
...WHY DOES THAT HAVE TO MEAN SAYING GOODBYE TO HIM?
THE PLACE HE'S IN NOW IS A VERY SPECIAL PLACE EVEN WITHIN THE SOUL SOCIETY.
ALTHOUGH...
...KNOWING HIM, I'M SURE HE'LL COME BACK SAFELY.
WHAT I'M WOR-RIED ABOUT IS...
...NOT KNOW-ING...
...WHAT KIND OF POWER HE'LL COME BACK WITH.
WHY IS THAT A PROBLEM ...?
DEPENDING ON THE TYPE OF POWER IT IS, IT MAY AFFECT THE WORLD OF THE LIVING.
IF THAT'S THE CASE...

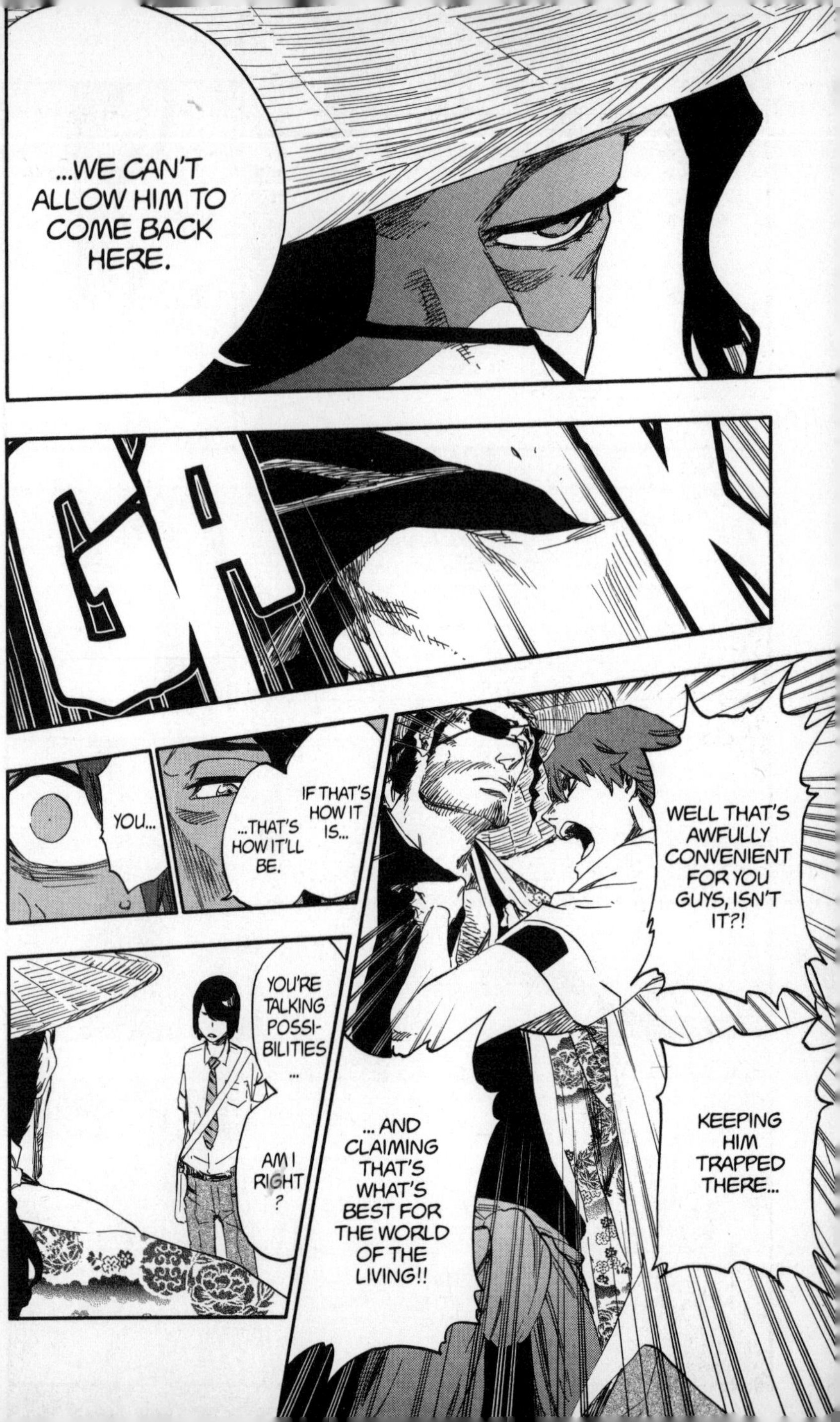
...WE CAN'T ALLOW HIM TO COME BACK HERE.
WELL THAT'S AWFULLY CONVENIENT FOR YOU GUYS, ISN'T IT?!
KEEPING HIM TRAPPED THERE...
...AND CLAIMING THAT'S WHAT'S BEST FOR THE WORLD OF THE LIVING!!
IF THAT'S HOW IT IS...
...THAT'S HOW IT'LL BE.
YOU...
YOU'RE TALKING POSSI-BILITIES...
AM I RIGHT?

READ THIS WAY

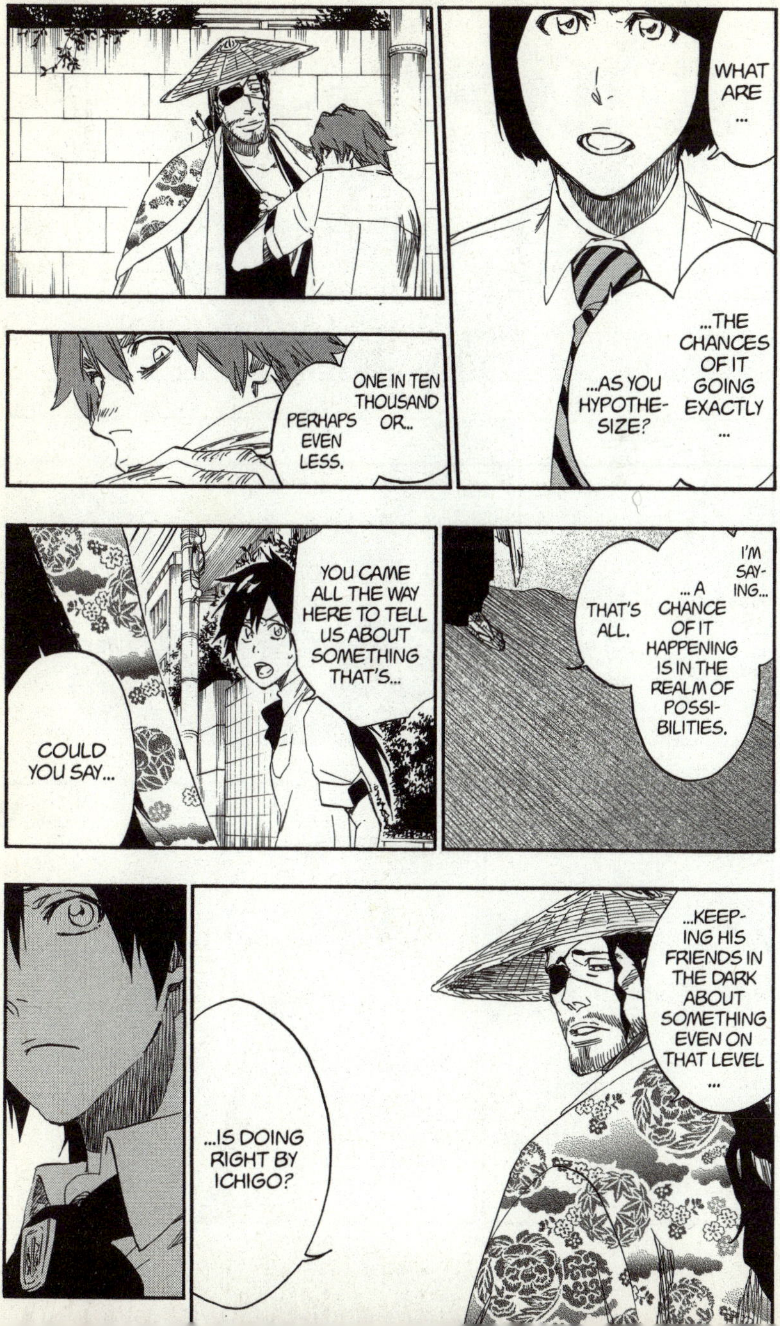

BA-M
AND SO...
HERE YOU GO!
WHAT'S THIS...?
THOSE ARE CALLED SOUL TICKETS.
IT'S A...
...TRANSIT PERMIT THAT'LL ALLOW YOU TO FREELY ENTER THE SOUL SOCIETY...
...IN CASE ICHIGO WON'T BE ABLE TO LEAVE.
UMM...
SHOULDN'T THESE BE...
DON'T WORRY.
I'VE ALREADY SENT SOME TO ICHIGO'S FAMILY.

IT'S STILL A WAYS DOWN THE ROAD.

IT'S NOT LIKE IT'S GOING TO BE TODAY OR TOMORROW.

DON'T LOOK SO SAD...

I'LL TELL HIM TO SPEND SOME TIME HERE UNTIL...

...THE BATTLE STARTS.

WHEN ICHIGO EVENTUALLY RETURNS...

...I'LL TELL HIM TO COME BACK HERE.

GULP
YOU TIRED, INOUE?
WANNA CALL IT A DAY?
NO.
I'M FINE.
I WAS JUST...
...THINKING HOW PEACEFUL IT WAS.
PEACEFUL?
YOU KNOW WE'RE TRAINING FOR A BATTLE, RIGHT?
TMP
WELL YEAH, BUT...

I JUST THINK... ...THAT'S KINDA NICE.

STILL... FOR US HUMANS TO BE IN HUECO MUNDO... HELPING THE ARRANCARS... WORKING HARD FOR THE SOUL REAPERS...

RESPECTING EACH OTHER'S WORLDS. ...HELPING ONE ANOTHER. EVERYBODY... ...COULD LAST FOREVER. I WISH IT...

THEN MAYBE... ...THE BATTLE WOULD NEVER START.

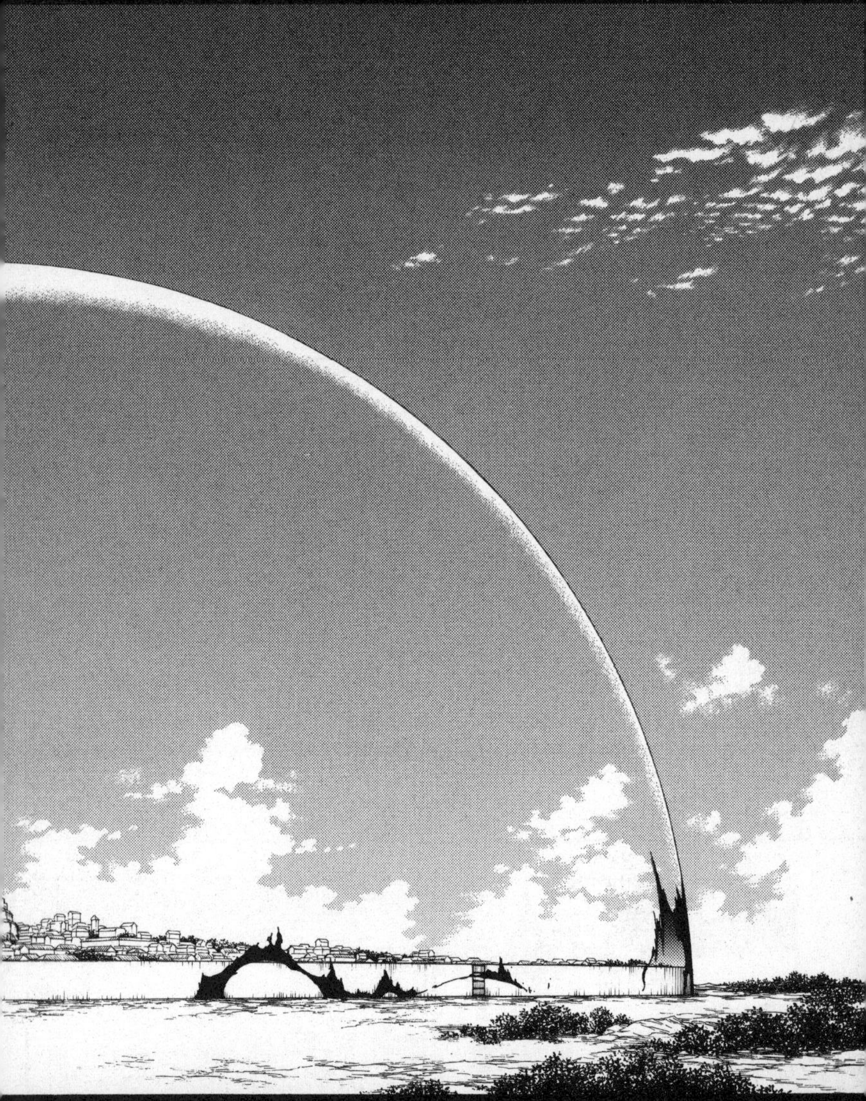

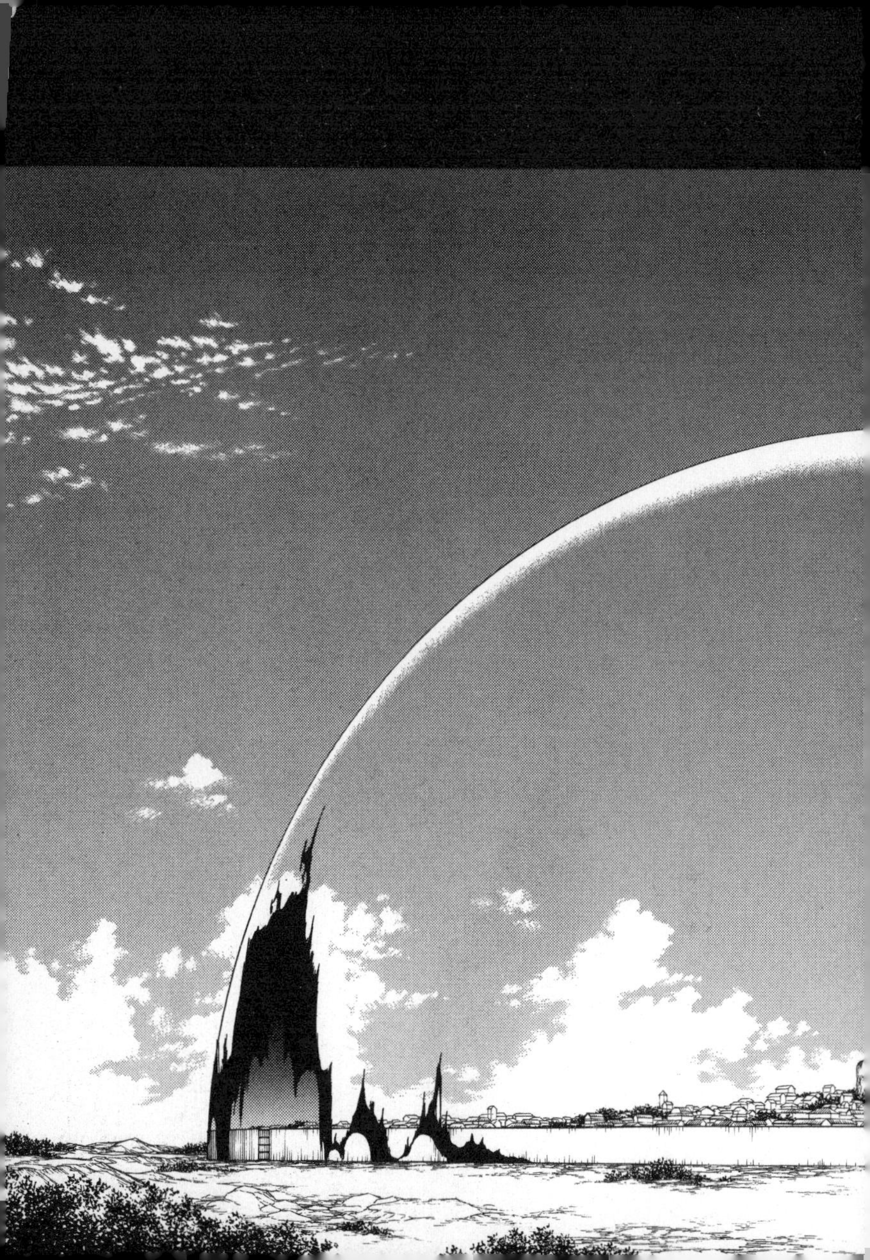

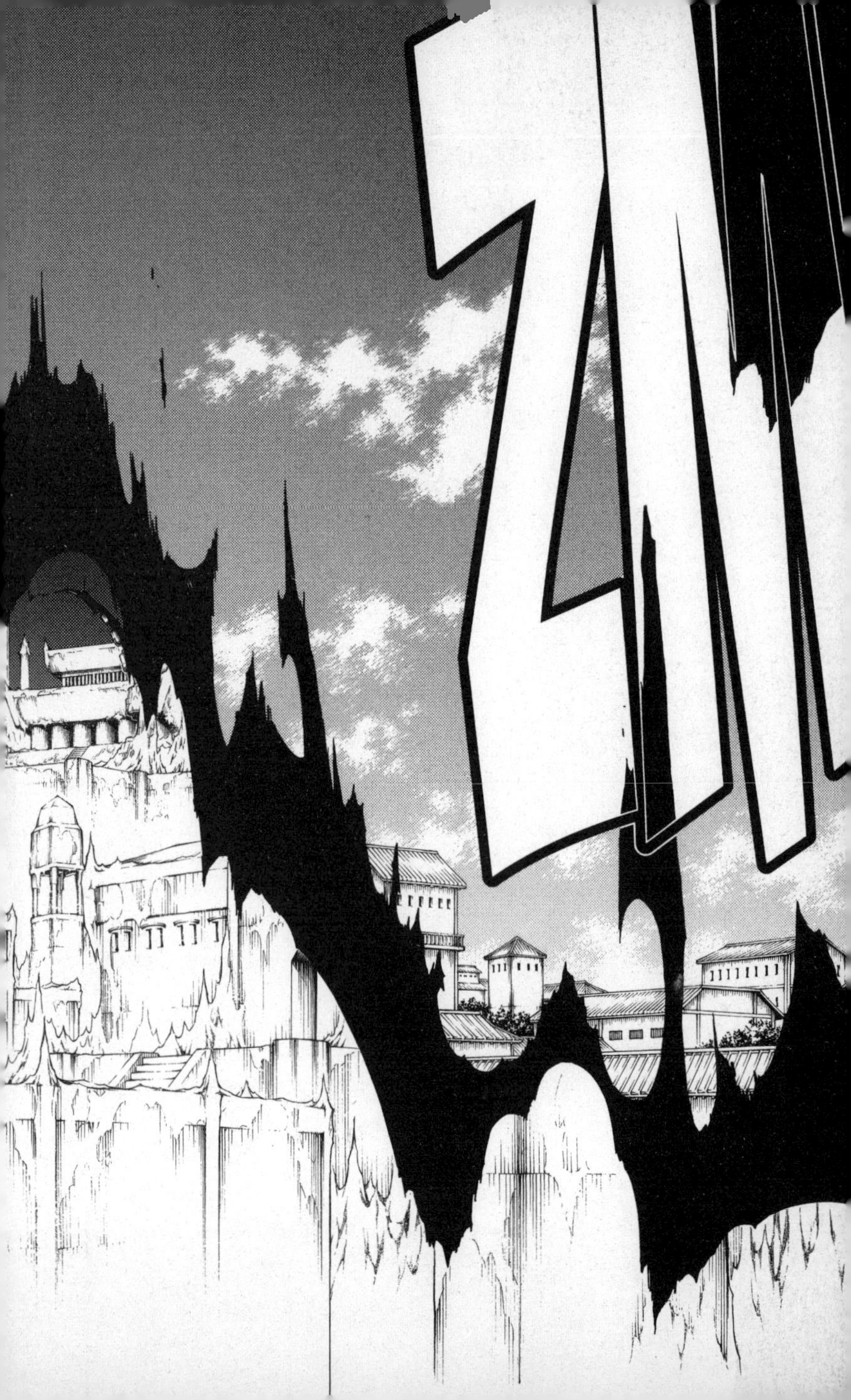

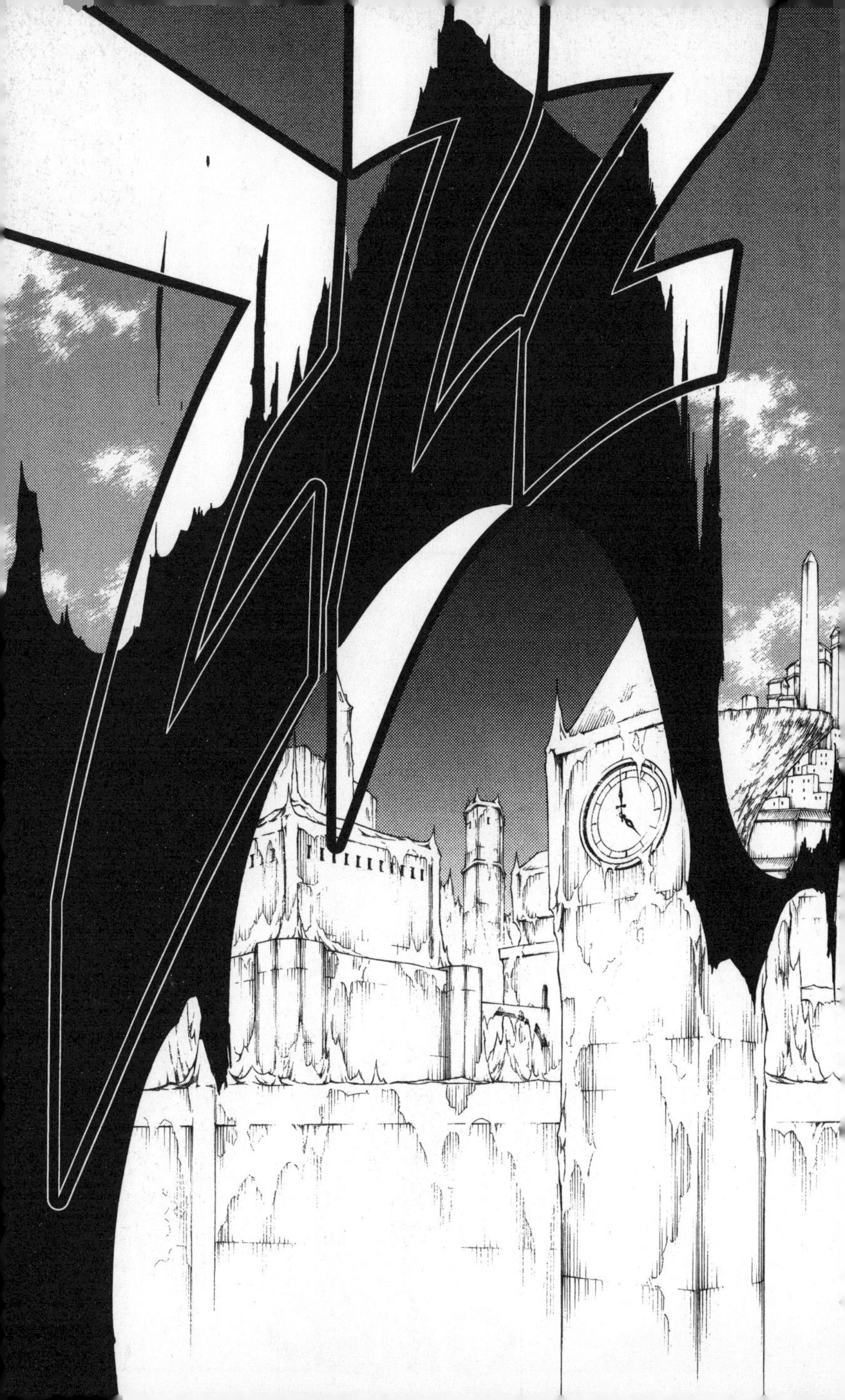

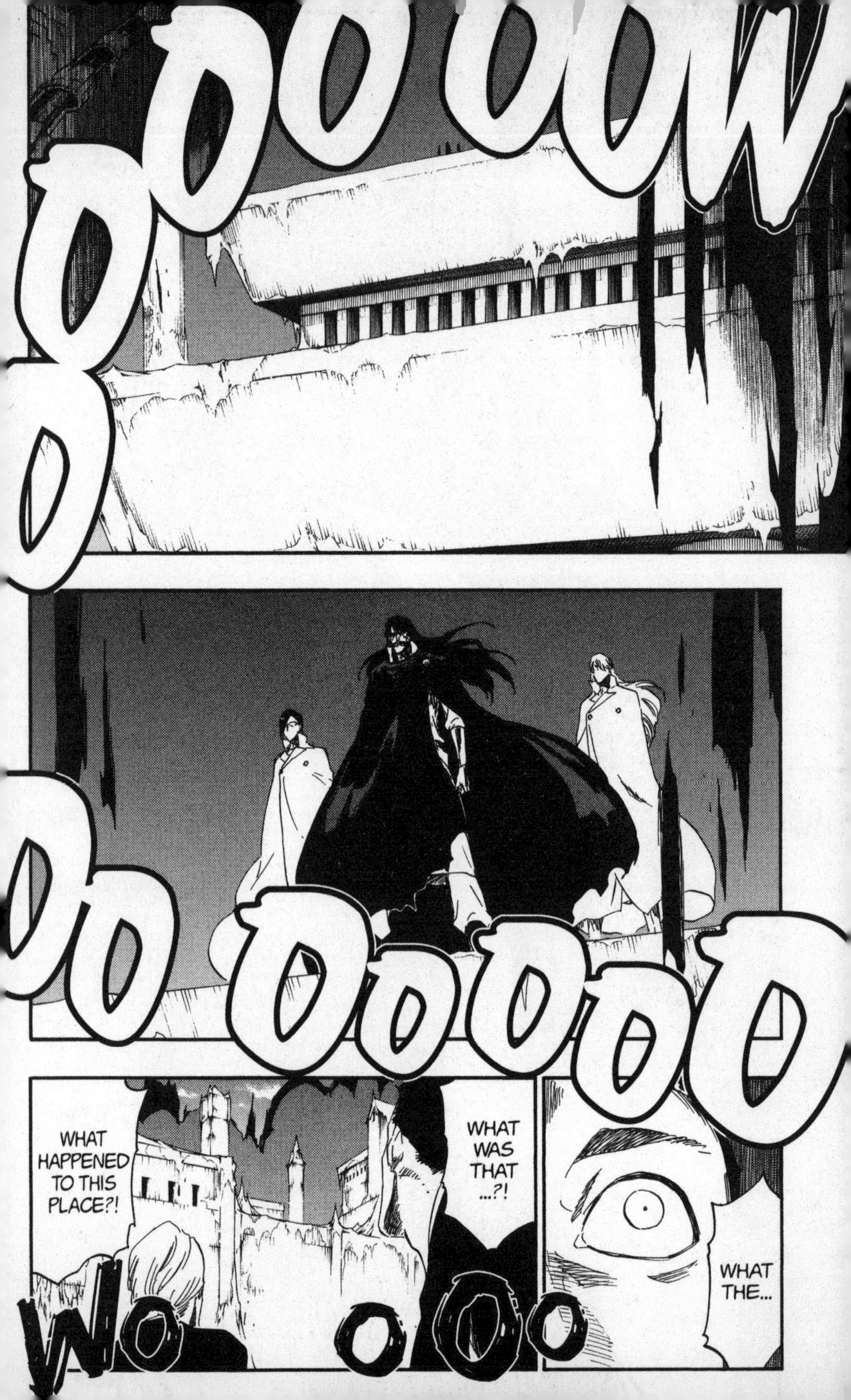
WHAT THE...
WHAT WAS THAT ...?!
WHAT HAPPENED TO THIS PLACE?!

THIS... THIS CAN'T BE...!!

I DON'T BELIEVE THIS...

WHAT'S GOING ON?!!

ALL THE METERS ARE GOING BERSERK!!

THE SEIREITEI IS...

...GONE!!!

...IS COMPLETE.

THE INVASION...

DO YOU KNOW THE KAISER GESANG?
(KING'S HYMN)

URYU.

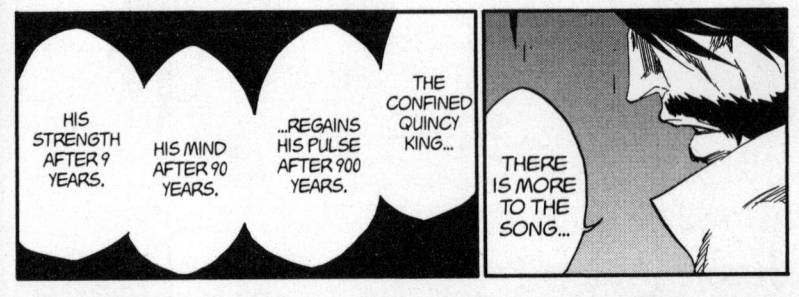

Panel	
HIS STRENGTH AFTER 9 YEARS.	HIS MIND AFTER 90 YEARS.

"HIS STRENGTH AFTER 9 YEARS."

"HIS MIND AFTER 90 YEARS."

"...REGAINS HIS PULSE AFTER 900 YEARS."

"THE CONFINED QUINCY KING..."

"YES."

"HIS STRENGTH AFTER 9 YEARS."

"HIS MIND AFTER 90 YEARS."

"...REGAINS HIS PULSE AFTER 900 YEARS."

"THE CONFINED QUINCY KING..."

"THERE IS MORE TO THE SONG..."

"AND THE WORLD IN 9 DAYS."

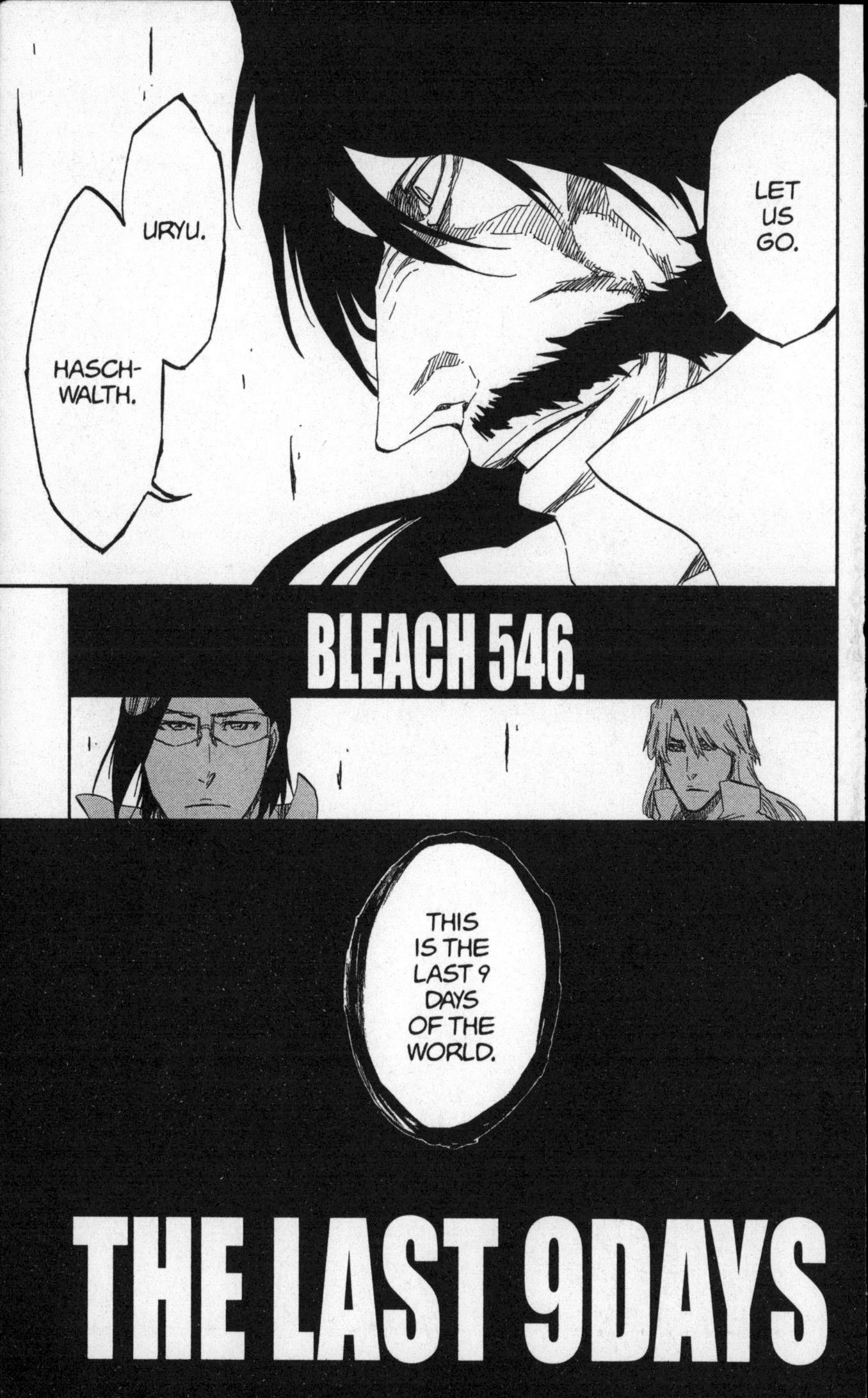
LET US GO.
URYU.
HASCH-WALTH.
BLEACH 546.
THIS IS THE LAST 9 DAYS OF THE WORLD.
THE LAST 9DAYS

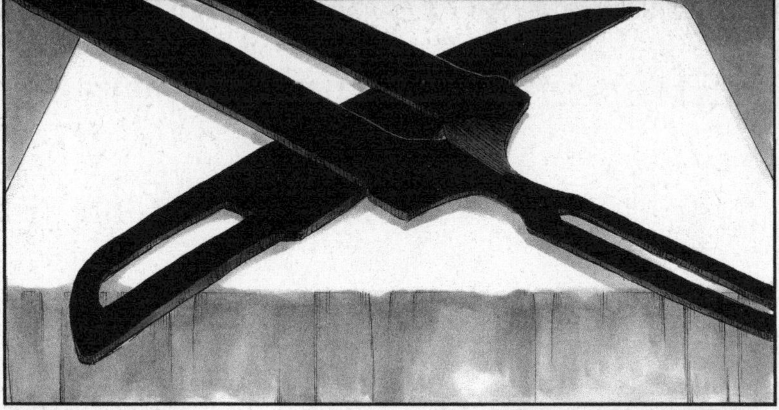

547. PEACE FROM SHADOWS

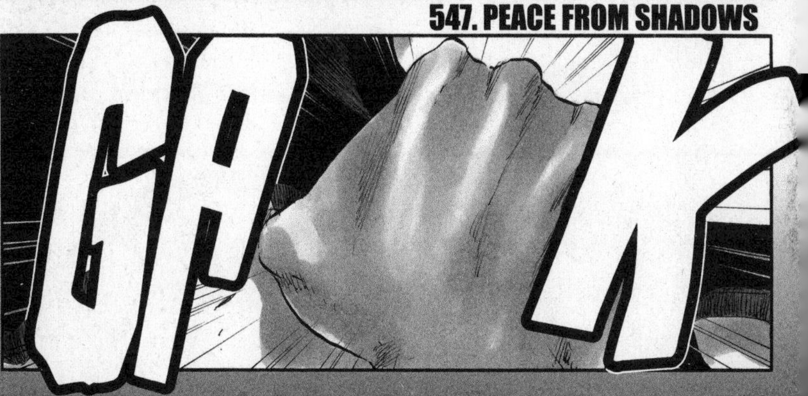
GAK

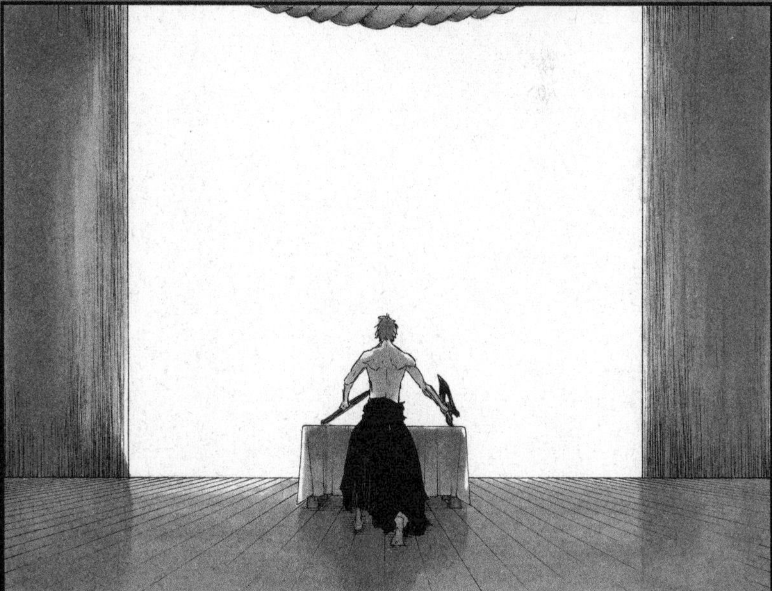

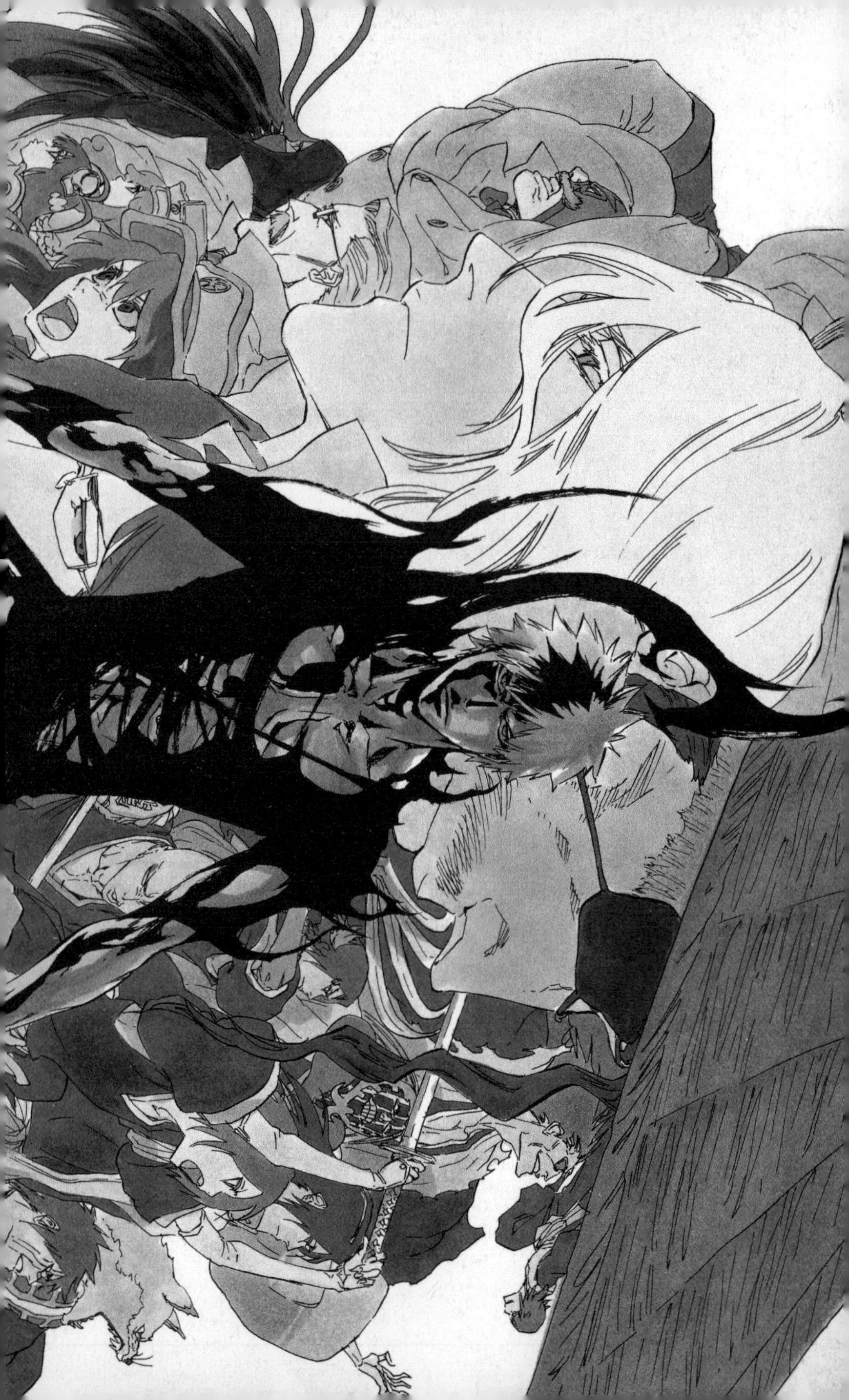

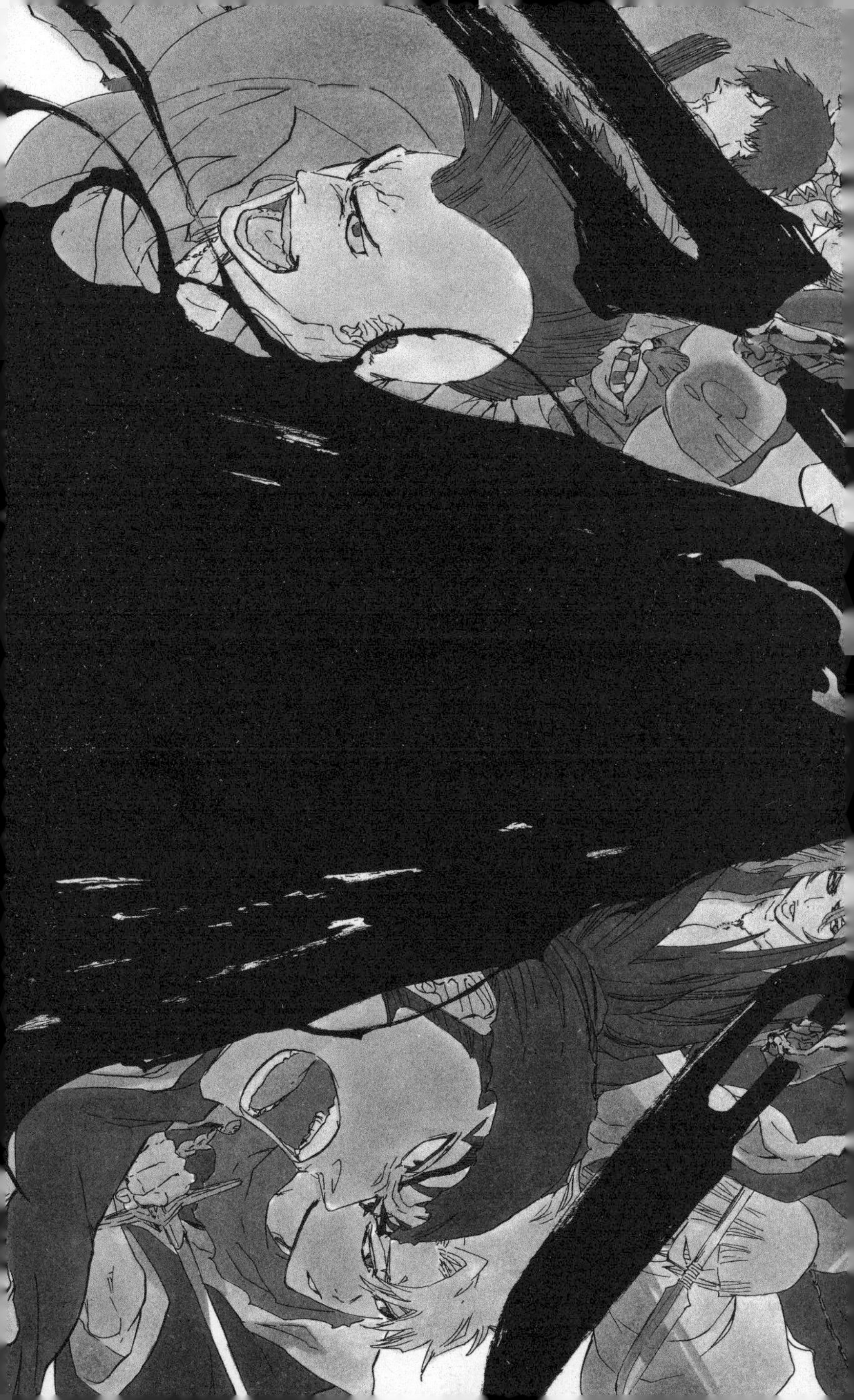

BLEACH
ブリーチ

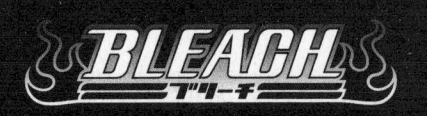

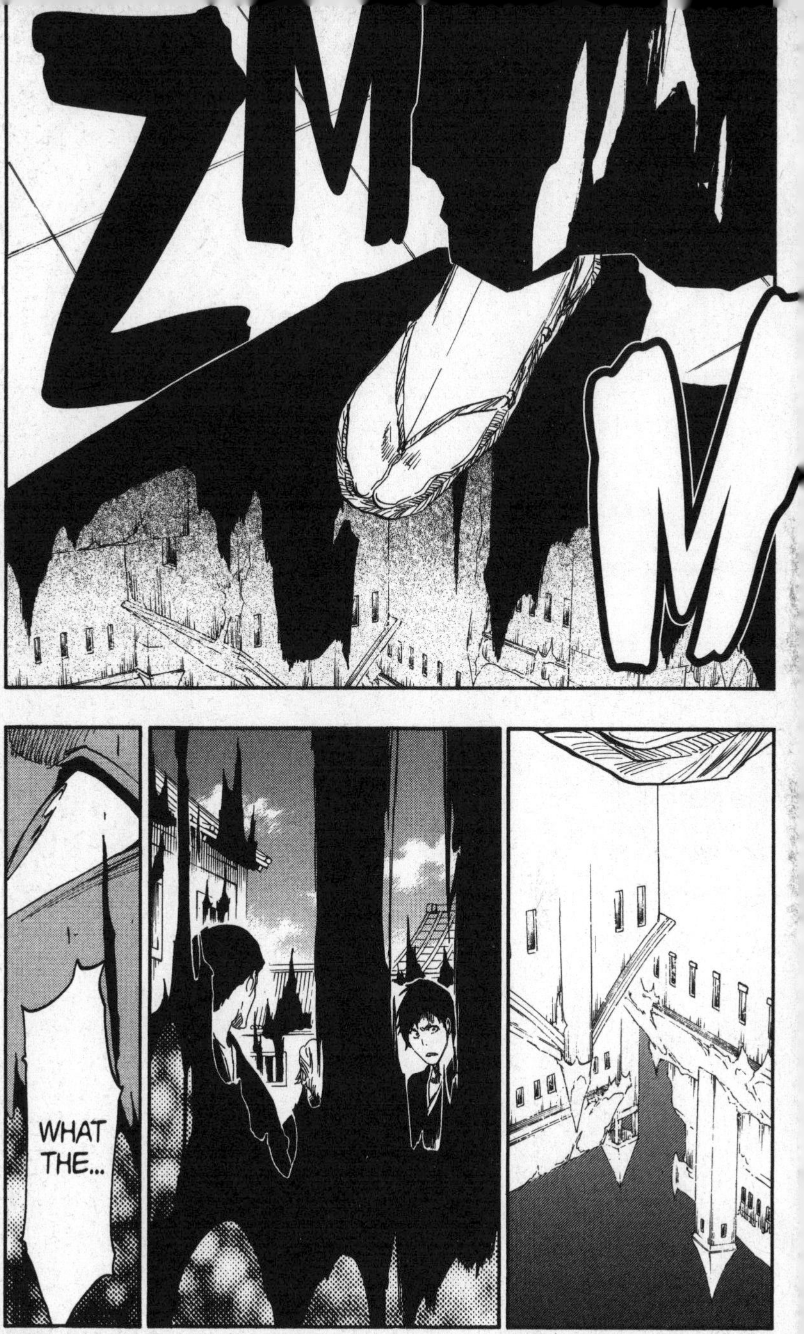
ZMMM
WHAT THE...

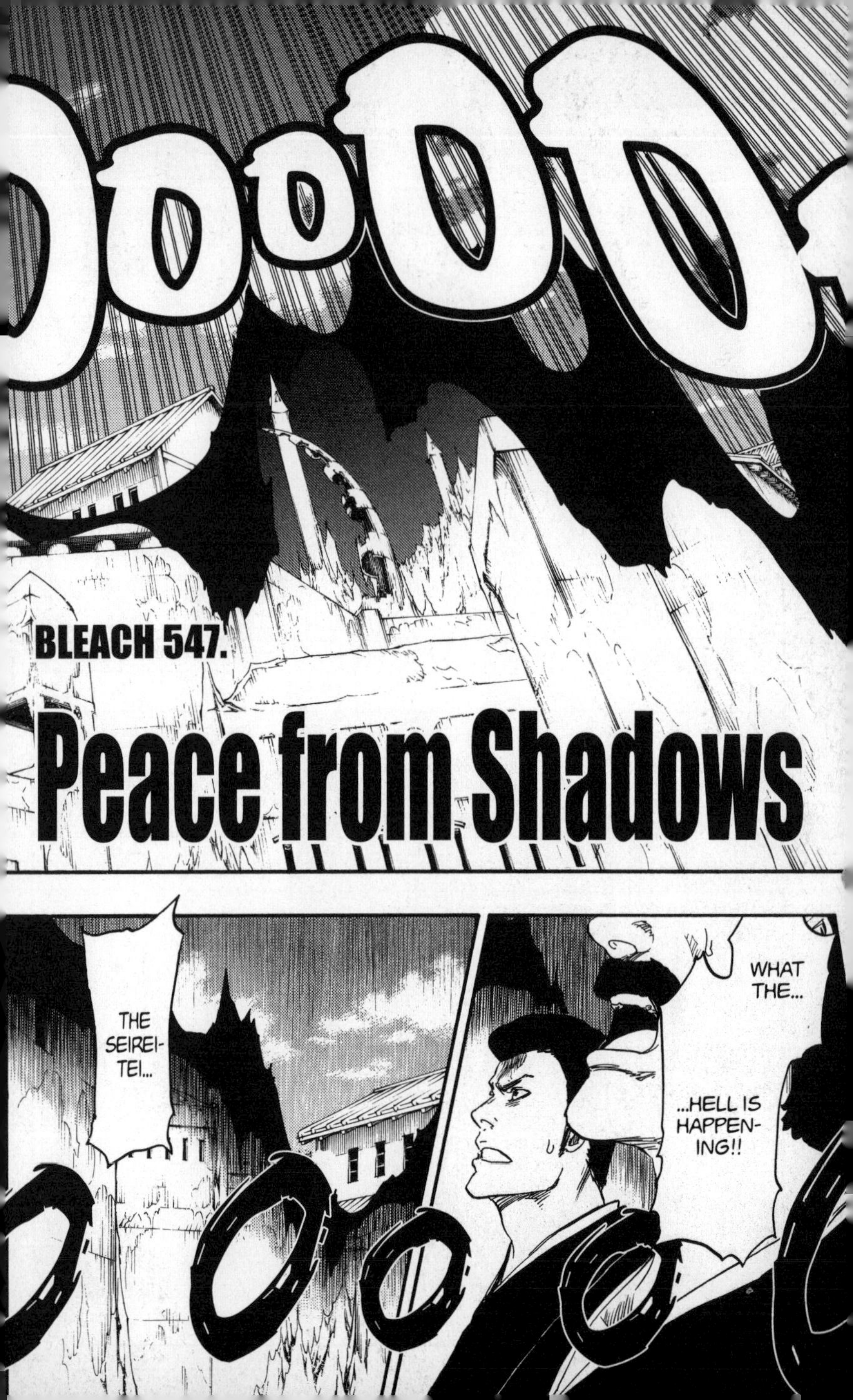
BLEACH 547.
Peace from Shadows
WHAT THE...
...HELL IS HAPPEN-ING!!
THE SEIREI-TEI...

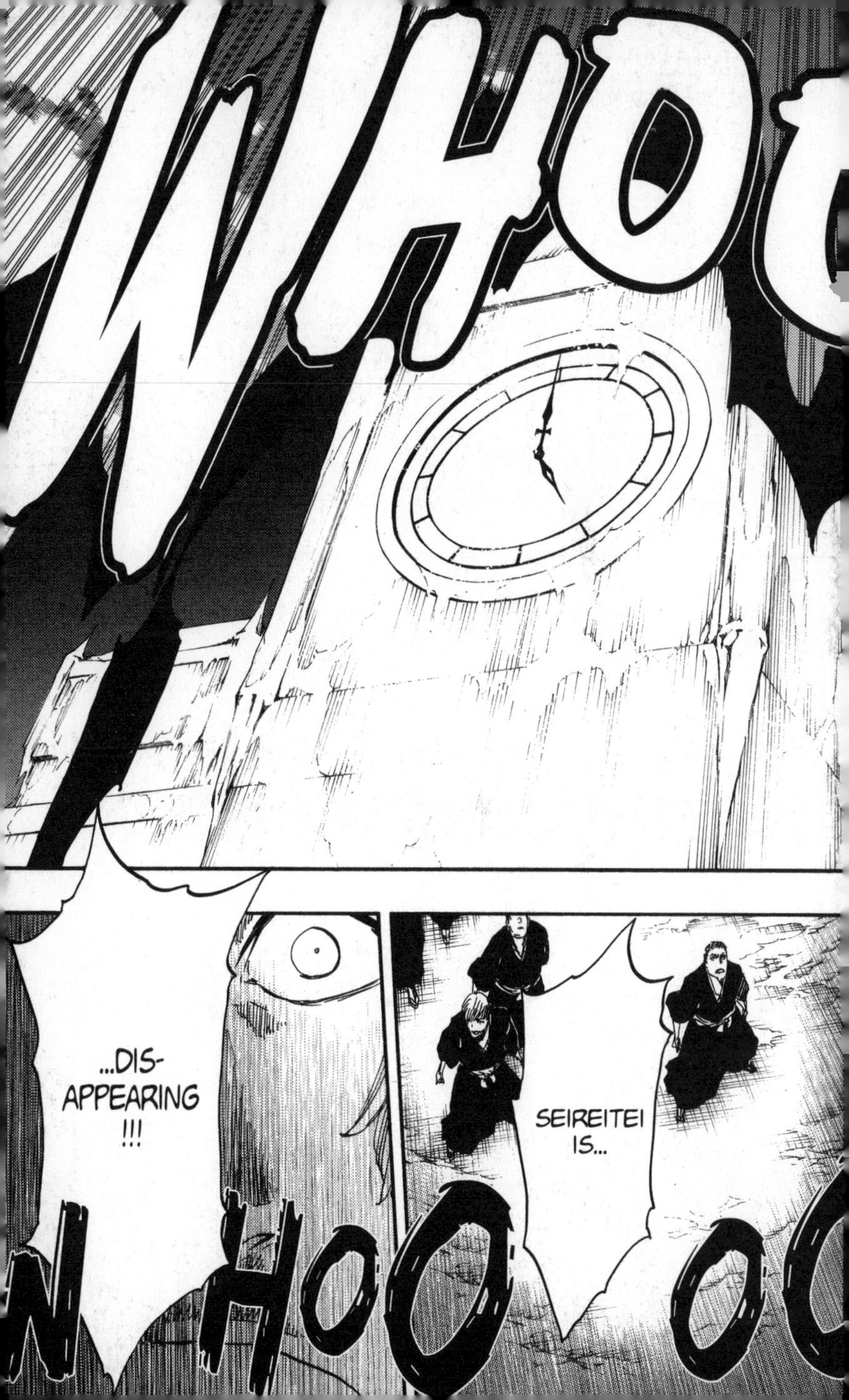
WHOO
SEIREITEI IS...
...DIS-APPEARING!!!
WHOOOO

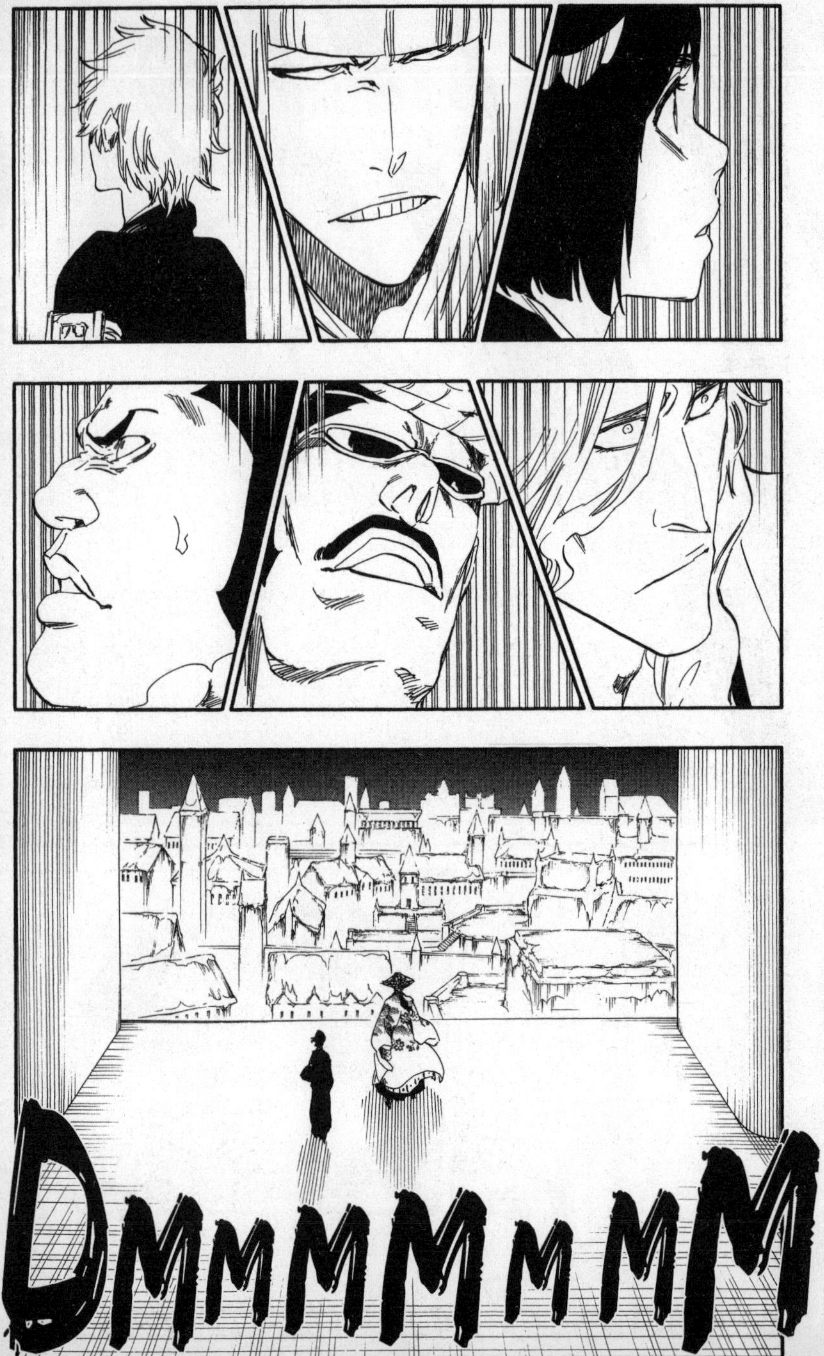
DMMMMMMM

READ THIS WAY

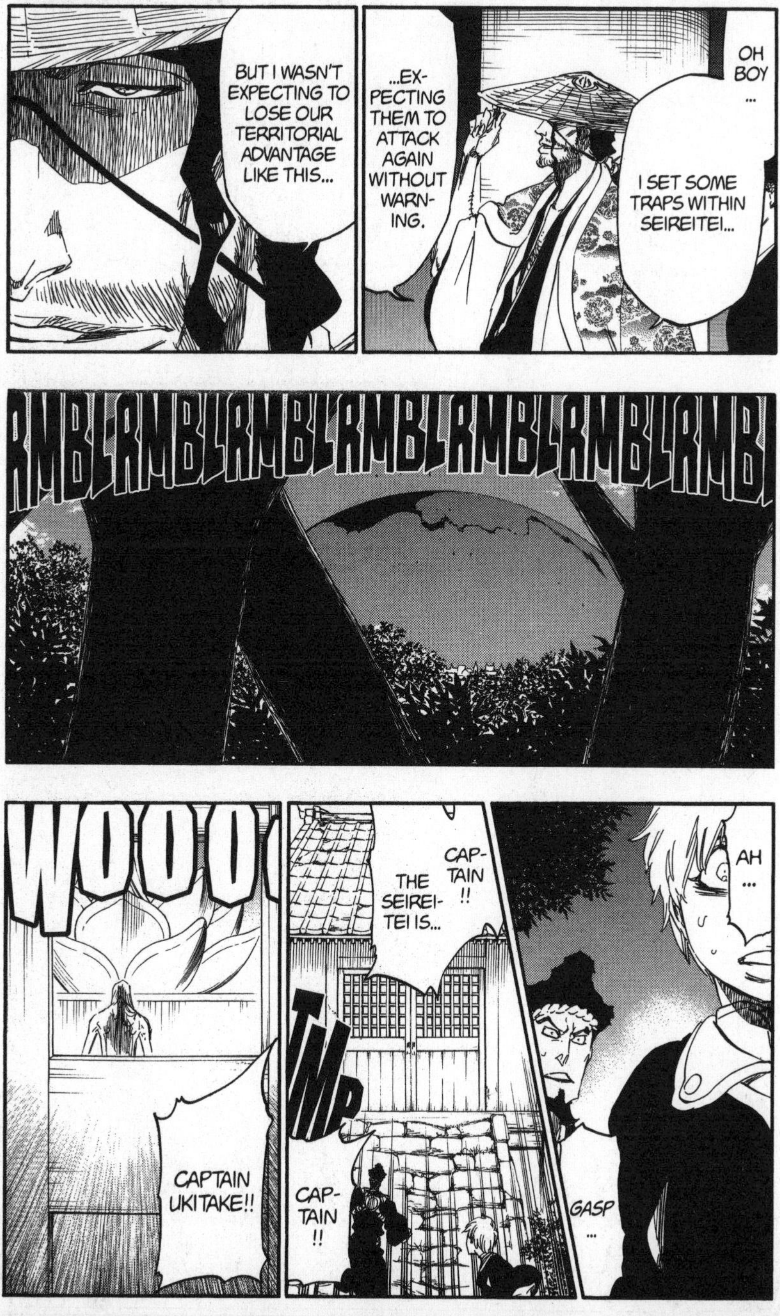

DAMN IT!
NOTHING'S SHOWING UP ON THE SCREEN!
DAMN IT!!
HIYOSU.
SHUT UP, AKON!!
SEIREITEI IS GONE ?!
YEAH RIGHT!!
ARE YOU DENYING THE INSTRUMENTS WE DEVELOPED OURSELVES?
YOU KNOW BETTER THAN ANYBODY.
THE NUMBERS YOU'RE SEEING ARE EVERY-THING.
WHAT ABOUT THE REALITY WE'RE SEEING WITH OUR EYES?!
THE INSTRUMENTS HERE HAVEN'T DISAPPEARED ...
BAM

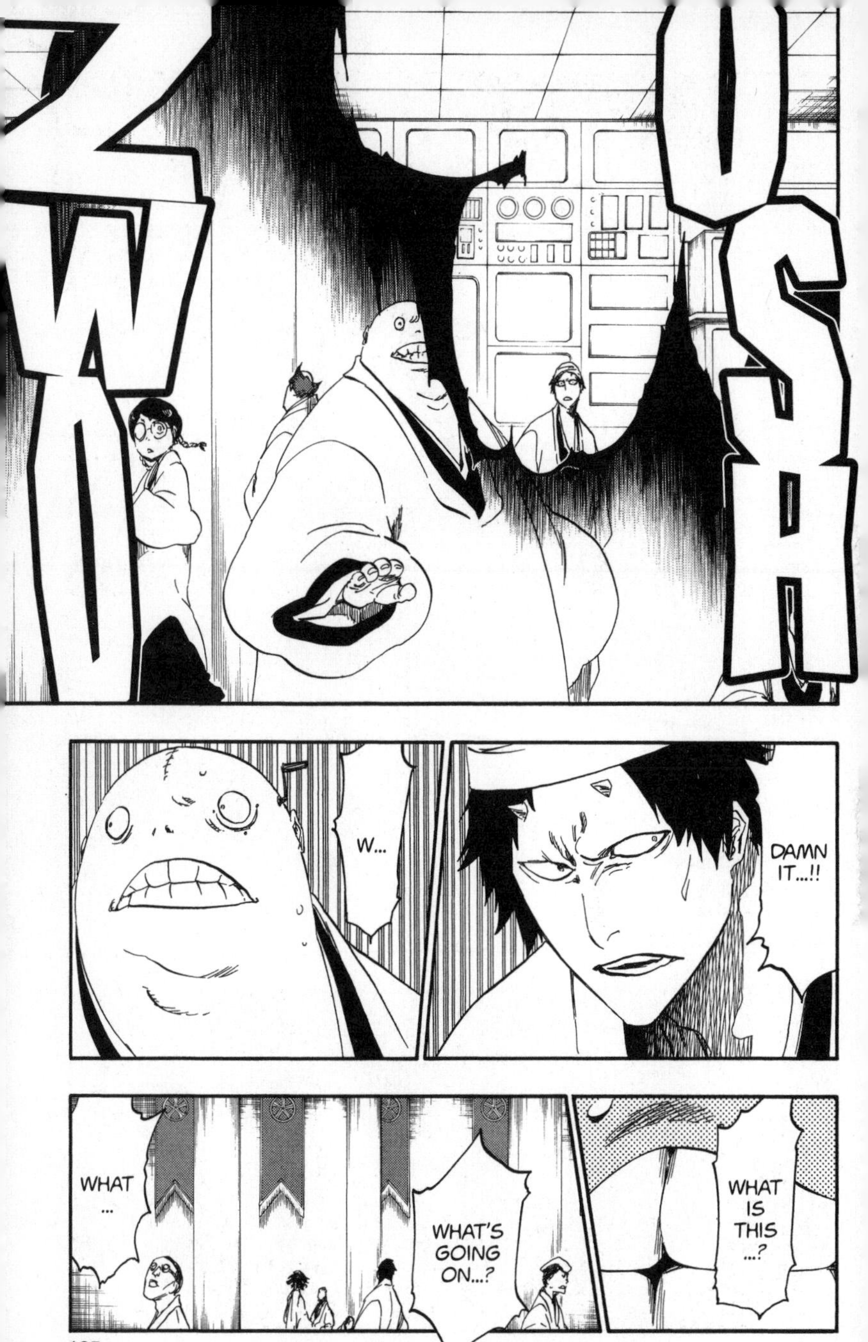
ZWUSH
DAMN IT...!!
W...
WHAT IS THIS ...?
WHAT'S GOING ON...?
WHAT ...

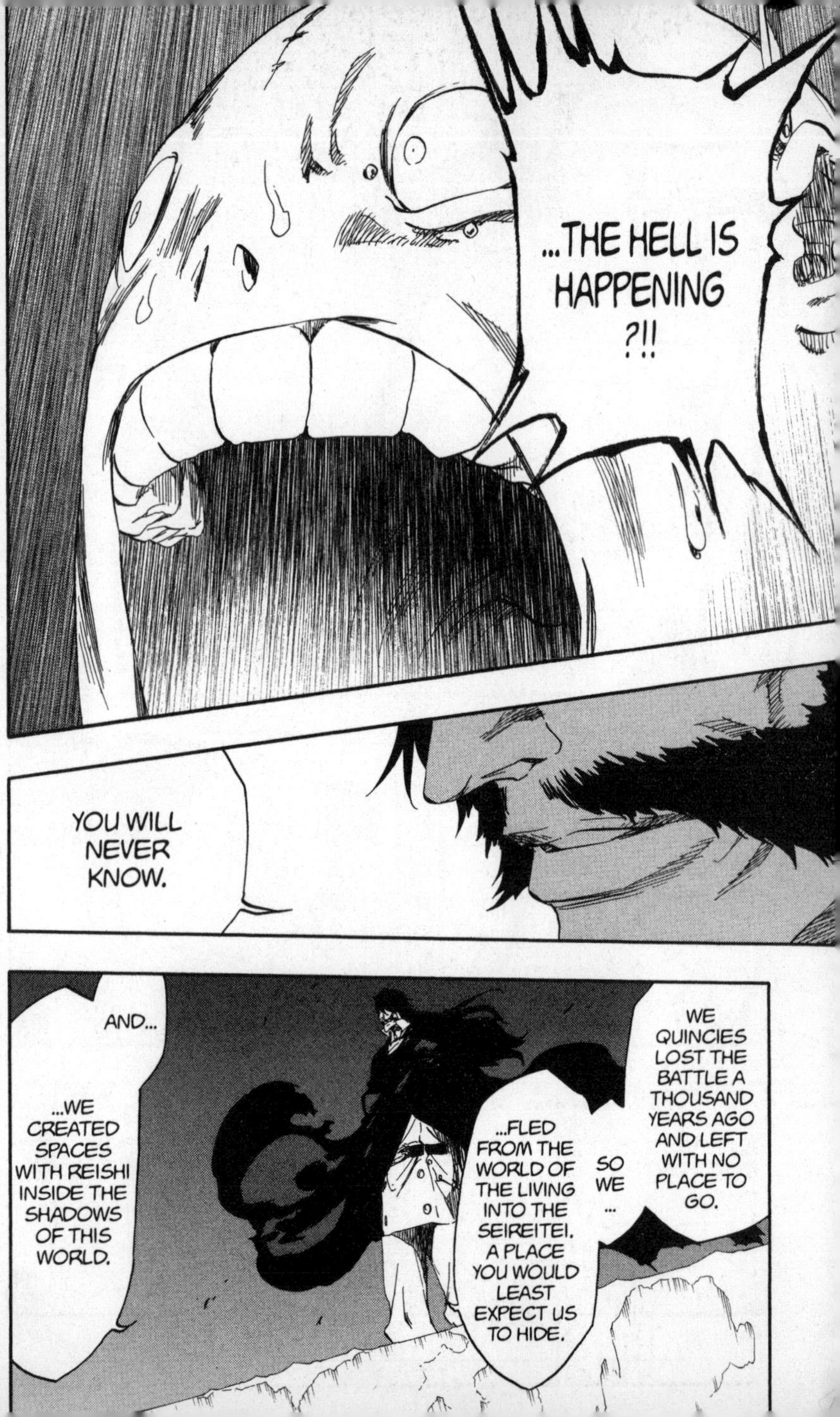
...THE HELL IS HAPPENING ?!!
YOU WILL NEVER KNOW.
WE QUINCIES LOST THE BATTLE A THOUSAND YEARS AGO AND LEFT WITH NO PLACE TO GO.
SO WE ...
...FLED FROM THE WORLD OF THE LIVING INTO THE SEIREITEI. A PLACE YOU WOULD LEAST EXPECT US TO HIDE.
AND...
...WE CREATED SPACES WITH REISHI INSIDE THE SHADOWS OF THIS WORLD.

THAT'S WHY WE CALLED IT...
...THE VANDENREICH, THE INVISIBLE EMPIRE.
THE PLAN WAS A SUCCESS.
UNLIKE THE WORLD OF THE LIVING, THE SOUL SOCIETY IS FILLED WITH REISHI, OUR SOURCE OF POWER.
THE THINGS WE COULD DO WITH IT WERE INFINITE.
!!
WE SPENT...
...A THOUSAND YEARS...
...BUILDING UP OUR STRENGTH FROM WITHIN THE SHADOWS.
TMP
IN OTHER WORDS...

TMP
...WE DIDN'T...
...INVADE SEIREITEI BY BREAKING THROUGH THE SHAKONMAKU BARRIER THIS TIME OR THE LAST TIME.
WE WERE ALREADY HERE TO BEGIN WITH.
!!
HI THERE ...
THANKS FOR THE VALUABLE INFORMATION.
IT DIDN'T TAKE LONG FOR YOU GUYS TO REACH WHERE THE CAPTAIN'S ROOM WAS.
IT SEEMS OUR ENEMY IS BLESSED WITH WELL-TRAINED MEN.

...JUGRAM HASCHWALTH.

VANDENREICH EMPEROR AIDE AND STERN RITTER GRAND MASTER...

OR DOES THE FACT YOU'RE HERE MEAN YOU KNEW?

I'VE JUST BEEN APPOINTED, SO YOU PROBABLY DIDN'T KNOW THAT...

THIRTEEN COURT GUARD SQUAD CAPTAIN GENERAL AND SQUAD ONE COMPANY CAPTAIN SHUNSUI KYORAKU.

OUR EMPEROR IS A LOVER OF PEACE.

HE BELIEVES THE SHORTER THE BATTLE, THE BETTER IT IS.

THERE-FORE HE ISSUED ONLY ONE ORDER.

HOW IMPATIENT OF YOU.

DON'T YOU WANT TO... ...ENJOY THE BATTLE YOU'VE BEEN WAITING A THOUSAND YEARS FOR?

YES.

THAT IS WHY I CAME HERE FIRST.

"EXTER-MINATE..."

"...THE ENEMY INSTANTLY."

I SEE...

WOOOOOOO

...DID YOU GET IN HERE?!

HOW THE HELL...

WHO ARE YOU...?

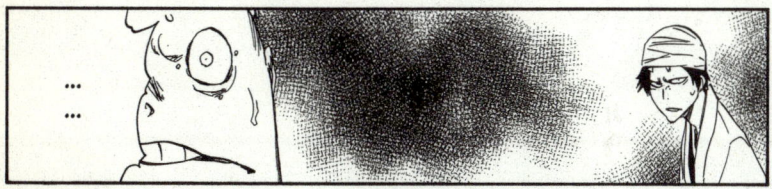

...BEEN HERE FROM THE BEGINNING.

WE'VE... WE DIDN'T GET IN HERE FROM ANYWHERE.

OR IS THE RESEARCH AND DEVELOPMENT DEPARTMENT ONLY CLEVER IN NAME?

WHOA, WHOA, WHOA. DIDN'T YOU LISTEN TO MY EXPLANATION?

...

CLNK..

EXACTLY.

TMP

HOWEVER...

CREATING ANOTHER WORLD INSIDE THE SHADOWS IS UTTERLY INCONSIDERATE...

OH MY...

PSsSSSH...

THEY JUST NEVER CAME IN CONTACT WITH ONE ANOTHER.

YOU QUINCIES WERE IN THE SHADOWS. TWO WORLDS EXISTED SIMULTANEOUSLY IN THE SAME PLACE.

FLAAAASH

...INCONSIDERATE THINGS.

...I DON'T HATE...

WITH THE DATA I COLLECTED DURING OUR BATTLE...

...I PREDICTED SHADOWS WERE RELATED TO YOUR INVASION.

WHAT ARE YOU WEARING...?!

FLAAASH

C... CAPTAIN...!!

SO...

...TO NOT HAVE ANY SHADOWS.

THAT IS WHY... ...I MODIFIED THE INSIDE OF OUR LABS...

SPARKLE

...GO AHEAD AND TRY TO FIND OUT...
...IF WE ARE ONLY CLEVER IN NAME.
DMMMMM
D...
DAMN IT...
DON'T LET HIM THROUGH !!
DO NOT LET HIM THROUGH !!
KLANG KLANG
TMP

IT'S WAY BEYOND THE POINT OF LETTING US IN OR KEEPING US OUT!

HAH! DO NOT LET ME THROUGH?! ARE YOU STUPID?!

SEIREI-TEI'S GONE!

THE INVASION'S ALREADY COMPLETE.

YOU MAY BE RIGHT. IT MAY BE BEYOND LETTING YOU GUYS IN OUR OUT.

HOW-EVER...

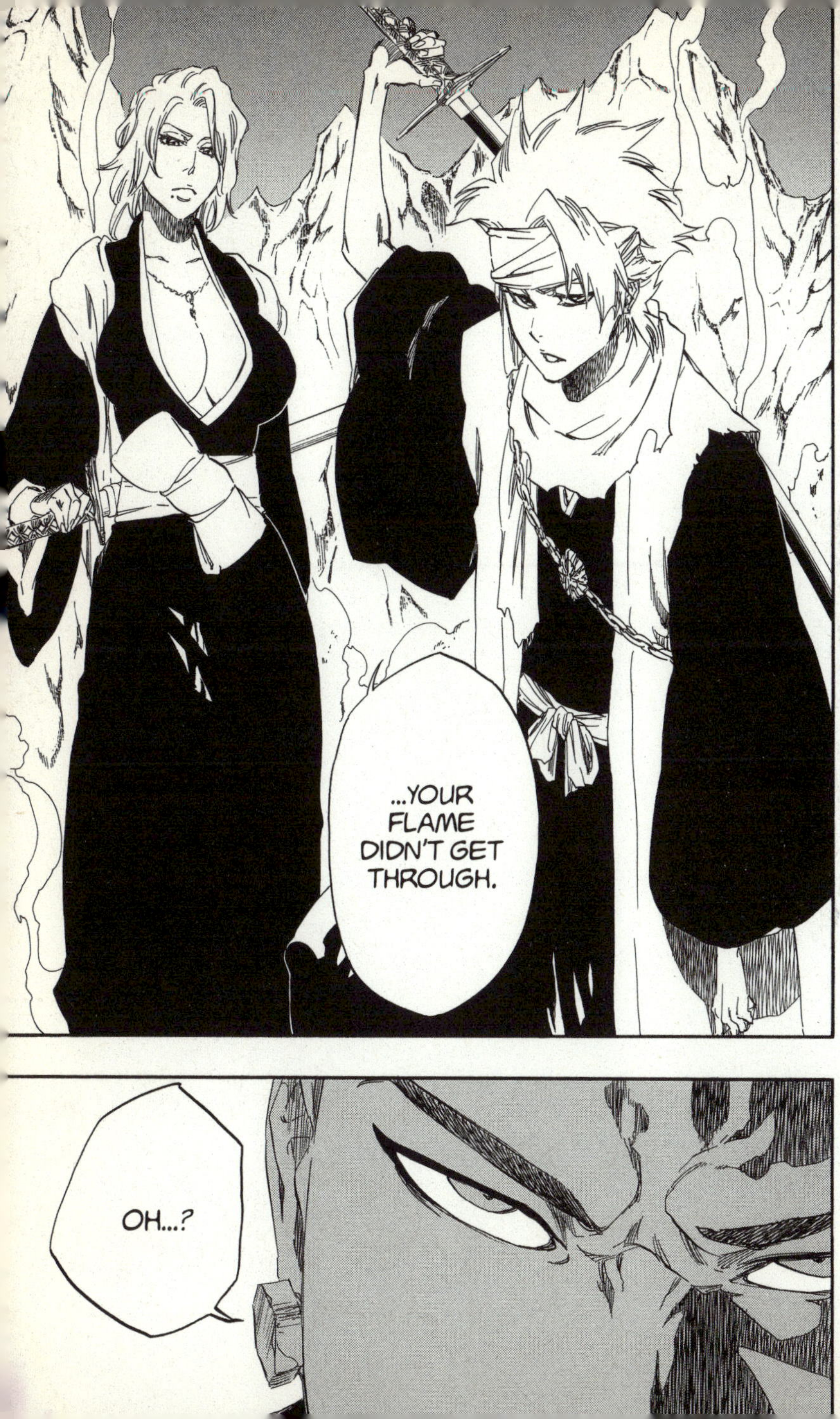
...YOUR FLAME DIDN'T GET THROUGH.
OH...?

DOOOOOOM

548. THE THIN ICE

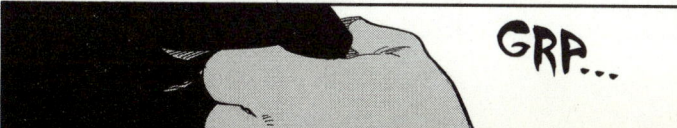

WAAAA

WHAT'S GOING ON...?! WHAT HAPPENED...?!

HURRY! GATHER AT THE BARRACKS!

WHERE THE HELL IS THE BARRACKS ANYWAY?!

WHAT'S GOING ON?!

I'M SCARED... SCARED, SCARED, SCARED!!

WHY DID THIS HAVE TO HAPPEN WHEN THE CAPTAIN'S NOT HERE?!

WHAT AM I SUPPOSED TO DO?!!

WHY DID THE MANSION DISAPPEAR?!

GRP...

BIG BROTHER...
MUST YOU GO...?
PLEASE DO NOT GO...
MAREYO IS FRIGHTENED...
YOU DO NOT HAVE TO PLAY WITH ME ANYMORE...
JUST PLEASE STAY HERE...

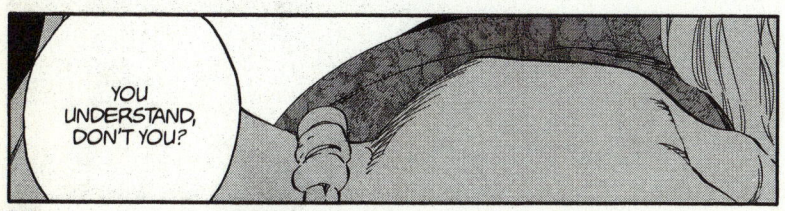

"I HAVE TO GO."

"NO."

"MAREYO. I KNOW YOU'RE SMART ENOUGH TO UNDERSTAND."

"YOUR BROTHER IS NOT LEAVING HERE TO SCARE YOU."

"BROTHER..."

"IN ORDER TO PROTECT YOU..."

"...SABURO, OUR SISTER, FATHER, AND MOTHER."

"OUR NEIGHBOR GONDAWARA AND KANEMITSU."

"AND..."

"...THE SEIREITEI."

"THAT'S WHY I MUST GO."

"YOU UNDERSTAND, DON'T YOU?"

...IS A MEMBER OF THE THIRTEEN COURT GUARD SQUADS.

BECAUSE YOUR BROTHER...

I'LL BE BACK SOON...

H-HEY! DON'T GIMME THAT LOOK!

GSHNK

KYUUUUU   UUU

SQK SQK SQK   SQK...

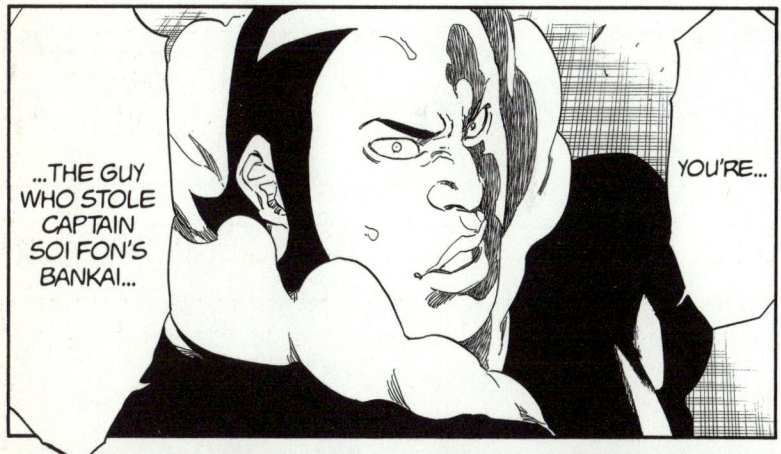

...THE GUY WHO STOLE CAPTAIN SOI FON'S BANKAI...

YOU'RE...

BLEACH 548.

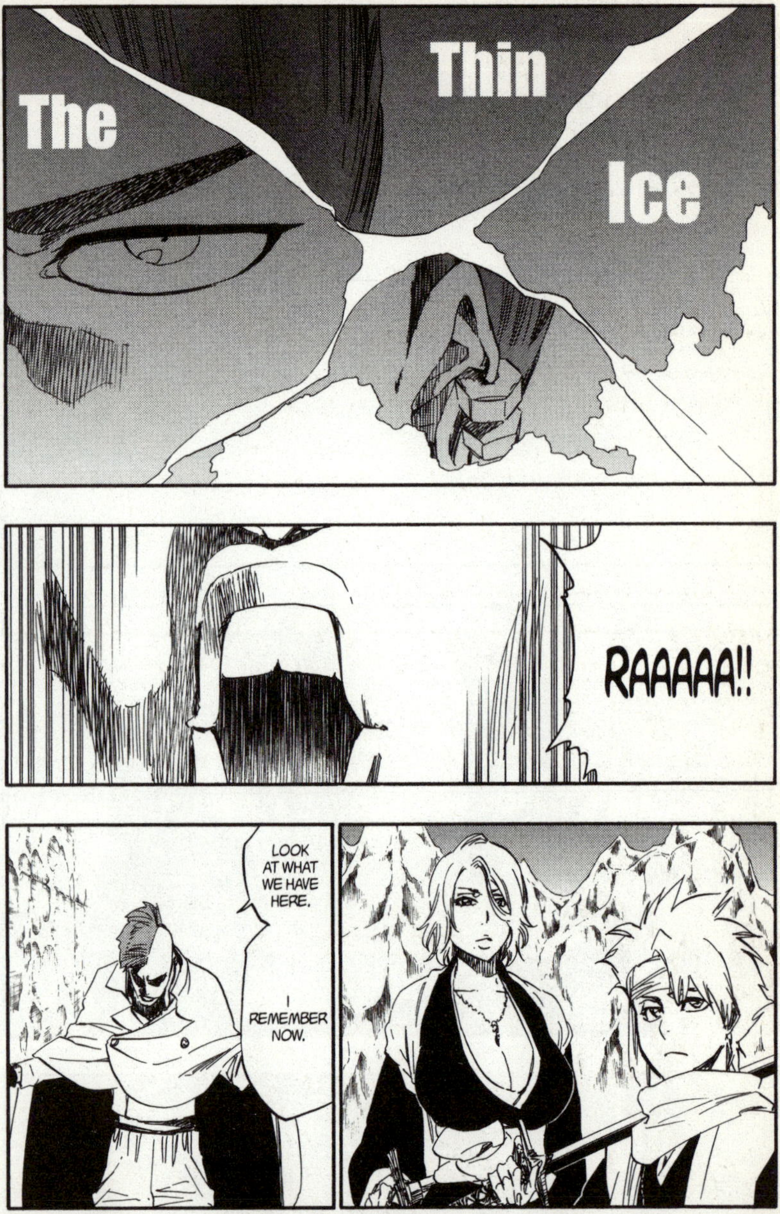
The Thin Ice
RAAAAA!!
LOOK AT WHAT WE HAVE HERE.
I REMEMBER NOW.

...WHO LOST HIS BANKAI TO CANG DU.

YOU'RE CAPTAIN ICE...

STERN RITTER "H"!

"THE HEAT"!

BAZZ-B!

SQUAD 10 CAPTAIN TOSHIRO HITSUGAYA.

WHOOOSH

SEEMS LIKE WE'RE A GOOD MATCH!

AN AWFUL GOOD MATCH!!

IT SEEMS SO.

AGH!
WHOA ?!
SH
!
FALL BACK AND PROTECT THE OTHERS!
THE CAPTAIN ...
...AND I WILL TAKE CARE OF HIM!

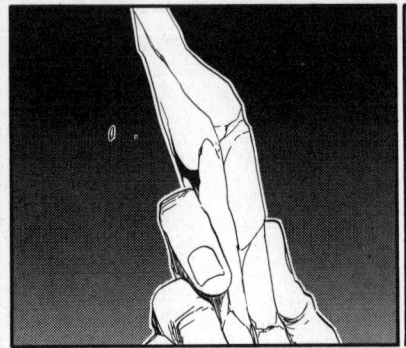

"HEY... LOOK AT THIS ICE..."

"Y... YES, MA'AM!"

"WILL HE BE ALL RIGHT...?!"

"CAPTAIN HITSUGAYA..."

"IT'S A MIRACLE THIS THING SAVED US FROM THAT FIRE..."

"THE ICE THAT PROTECTED US FROM THAT FLAME... IT'S SO THIN..."

"HEY, HEY, HEY, HEY!"

"WELL THIS ICE IS AWFULLY THIN!!"

WOOOOO

GWOOOOOF

READ THIS WAY

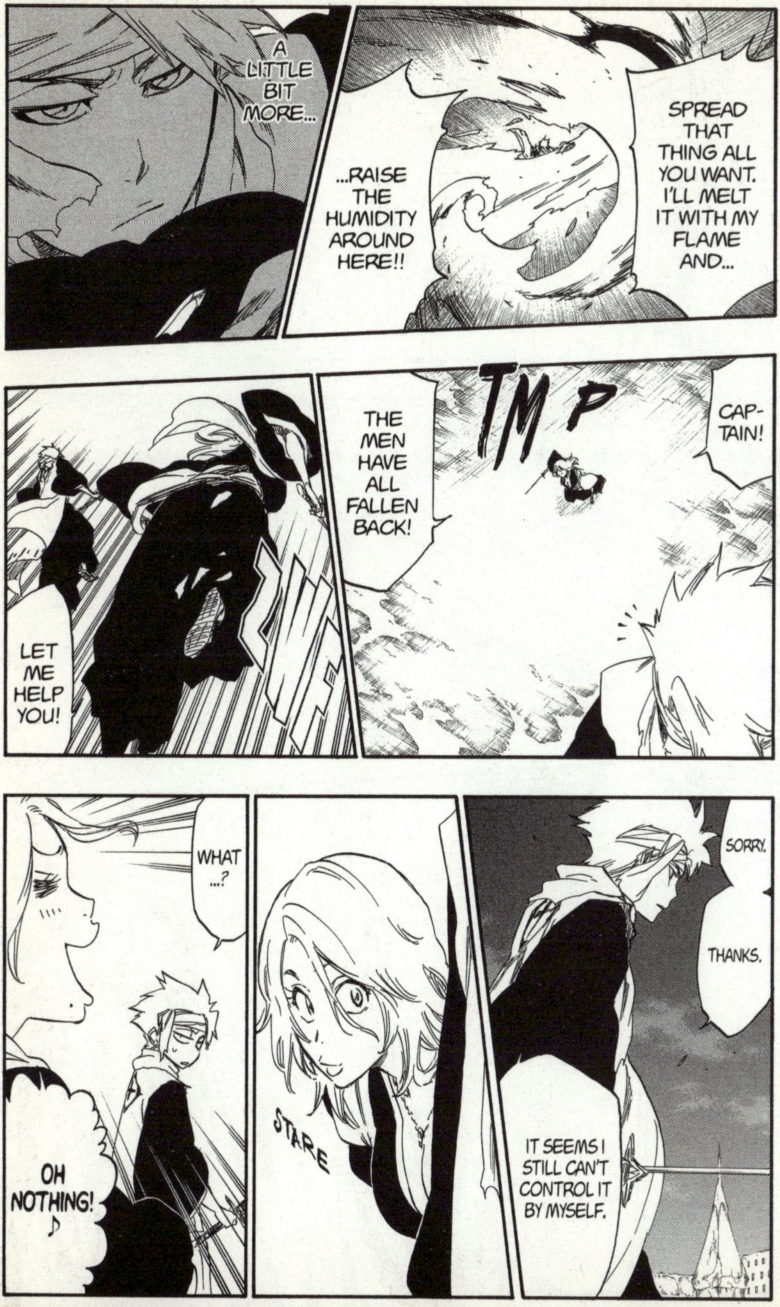

I WAS JUST THINKING...
...LOSING YOUR BANKAI WASN'T ALL BAD.
IT'S SO...
...CUTE THAT YOU'RE RELYING ON ME. ♪
WHAT...?!
MATSUMOTO!!
OKAY, OKAY. HERE I GO!
GROWL...
...HAINEKO!
OPERATION MILLE-FEUILLE!!
I NEVER GAVE IT SUCH A NAME!
WHAT NOW?

ZSSSH
CLN...K
JUST ANOTHER WALL OF ICE?!
HOW'S IT DIFFERENT FROM BEFORE?!
GWF
HAI-NEKO!
HOUSE!
FWP
DUMP
BOOOOF

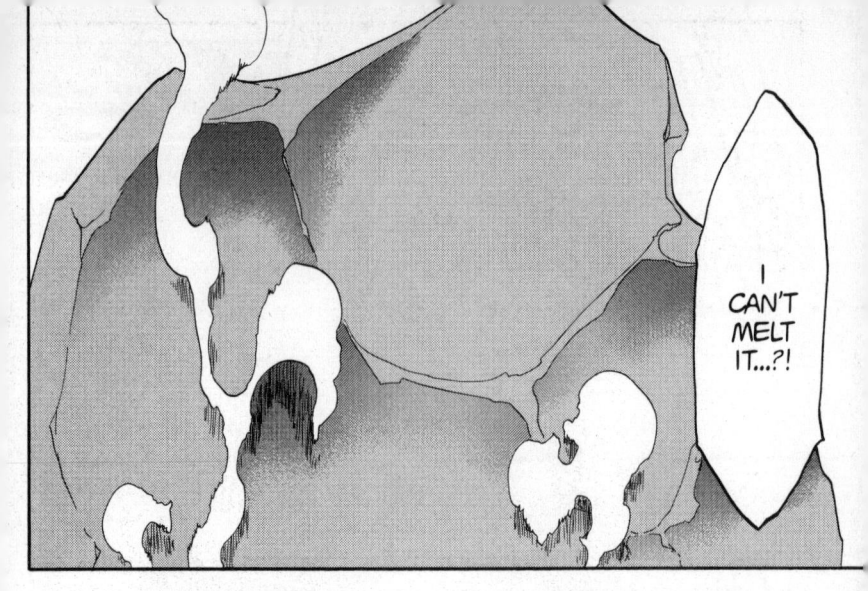

I CAN'T MELT IT...?!

IT'S A MULTI-LAYERED WALL OF VACUUM-ICE.

WHAT THE HELL...?

NO... THE SURFACE IS MELTED...

MY HYORINMARU IS PROBABLY THE ZANPAKU-TO...

...WITH THE LEAST AMOUNT OF DIFFERENCE FROM SHIKAI TO BANKAI OUT OF ALL CAPTAINS' SWORDS.

BY COVERING THE MULTIPLE WALLS CREATED BY HAINEKO WITH A THIN LAYER OF ICE AND ONLY RETRIEVING HAINEKO TO THE SWORD...

...MULTIPLE WALLS OF VACUUM-ICE ARE CREATED.

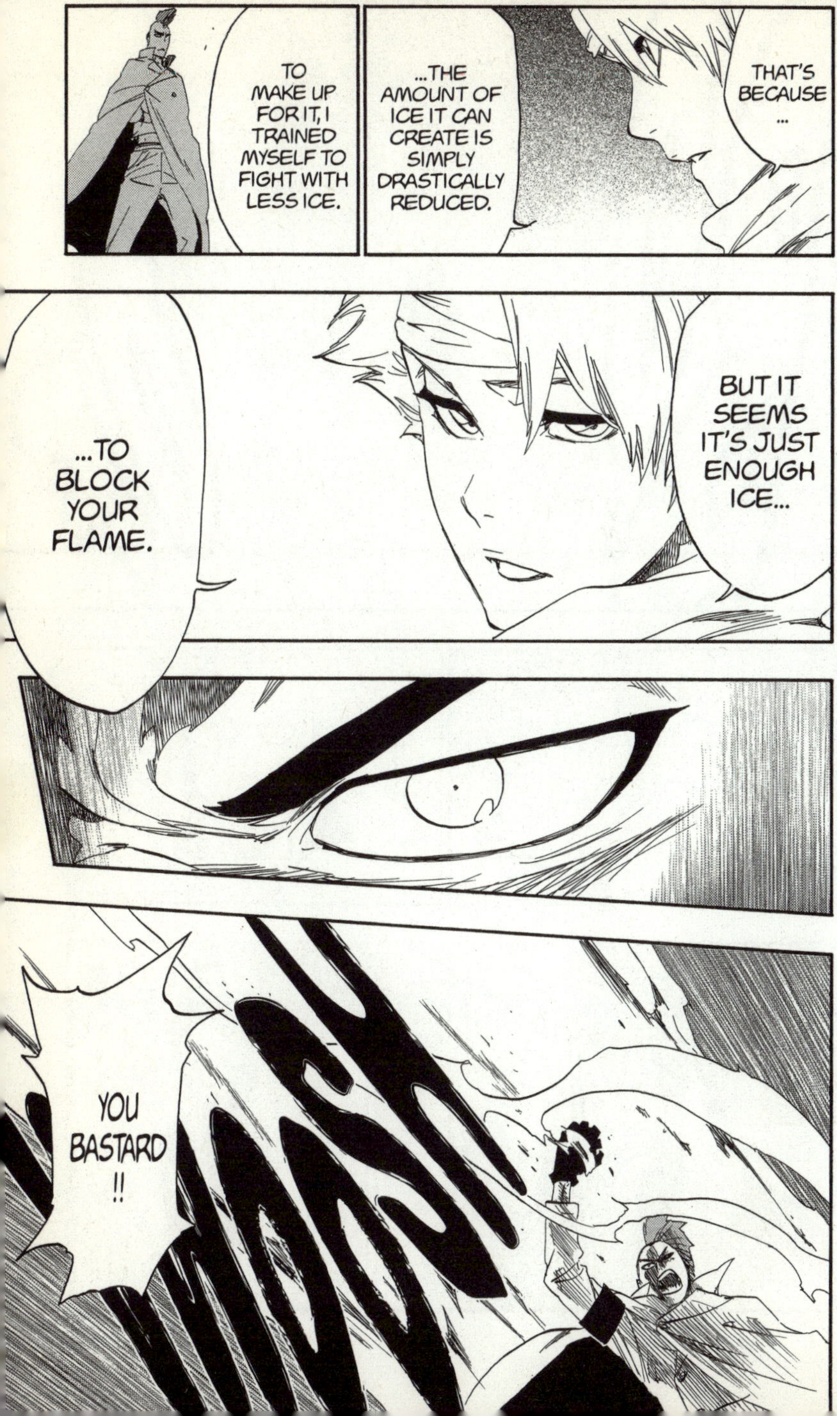
THAT'S BECAUSE ...
...THE AMOUNT OF ICE IT CAN CREATE IS SIMPLY DRASTICALLY REDUCED.
TO MAKE UP FOR IT, I TRAINED MYSELF TO FIGHT WITH LESS ICE.
BUT IT SEEMS IT'S JUST ENOUGH ICE...
...TO BLOCK YOUR FLAME.
YOU BASTARD!!
WHOOSH

YOUR FLAME...

...CANNOT PENETRATE THIS WALL OF VACUUM-ICE.

I TOLD YOU IT WON'T GO THROUGH.

NOW...

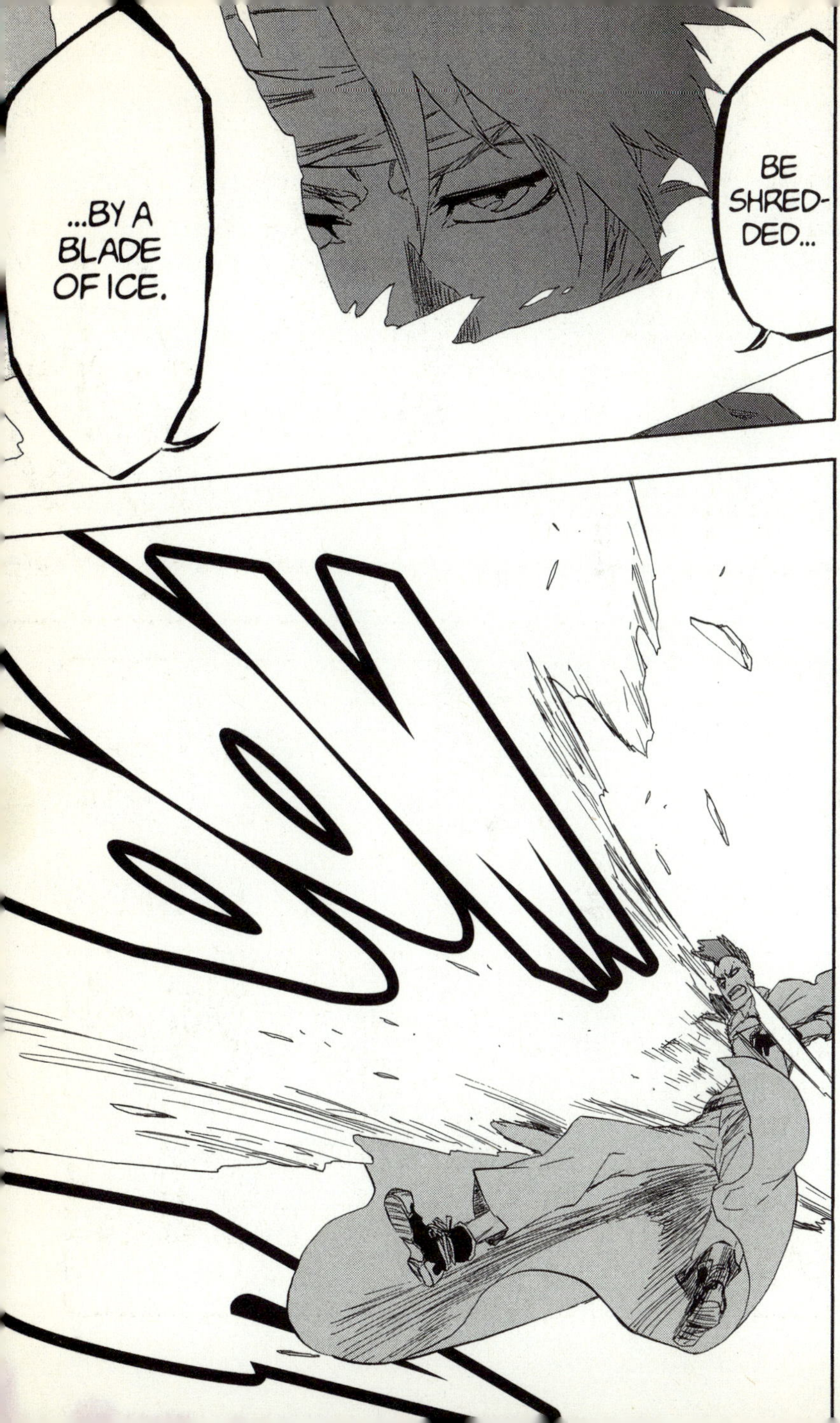
BE SHREDDED...
...BY A BLADE OF ICE.

BIG BROTHER

兄

CAPTAIN HITSUGAYA WON!!

HE BEAT HIM...!

WE CAN GO UP AGAINST THE QUINCIES WITHOUT BANKAI!!

WE CAN FIGHT THEM!

RAAAAAAAA

549. THE STORMBRINGER

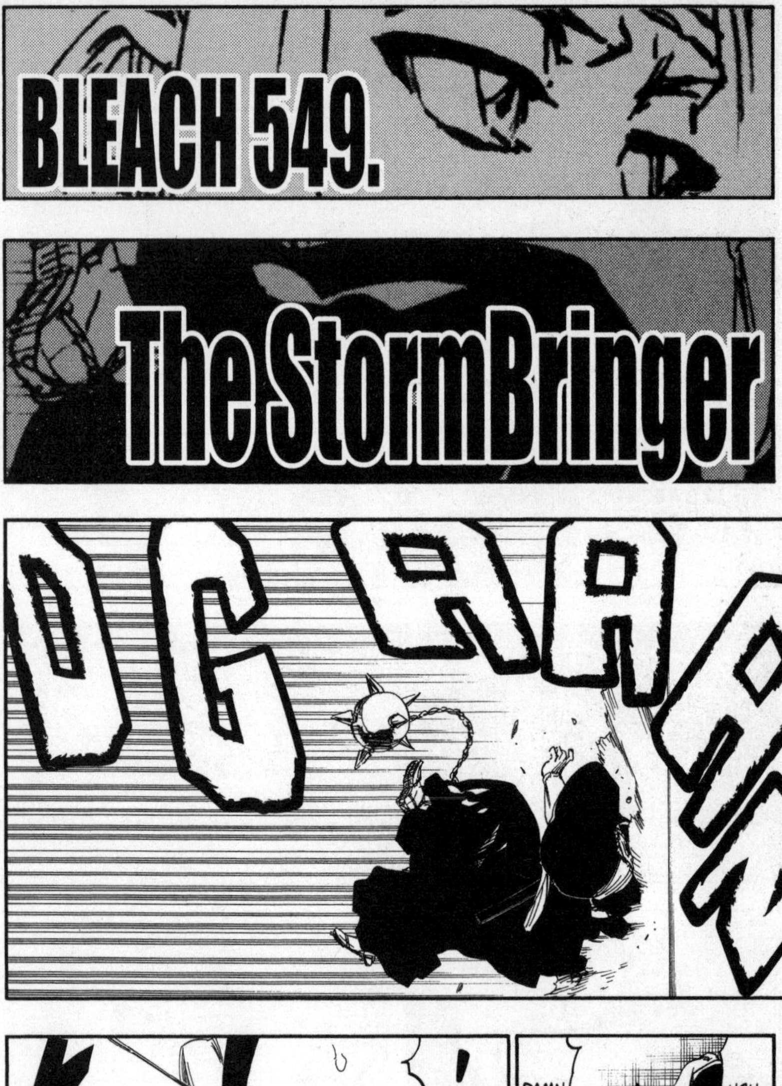
BLEACH 549.
The StormBringer
UGH...
DAMN IT...
!
KCHAK

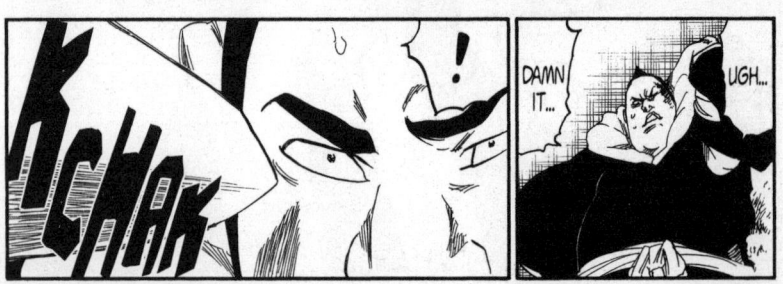

THIS IS MY THIRD TIME ASKING.

I AM HOPING FOR AN ANSWER THIS TIME.

WHERE IS YOUR COMPANY'S CAPTAIN?

SO YOU REFUSE TO ANSWER.

HOW SHOULD I KNOW...?

I EVEN EXTENDED THE SEARCH OUTSIDE THE SEIREITEI.

I SEARCHED THE AREA USING SPIRITUAL PRESSURE SAMPLES I ACQUIRED DURING OUR LAST BATTLE, BUT I COULD NOT LOCATE YOUR CAPTAIN.

...NOT TO GIVE UP THE CAPTAIN'S WHEREABOUTS, I'M THE KINDA GUY WHO'D LET IT SLIP OUT!!

IF I'M TOLD...

YOU DON'T KNOW MY PERSONALITY, DO YOU?!

SHE DIDN'T TELL ME!!!

USUALLY IN THESE SITUATIONS PEOPLE WON'T TELL YOU EVEN IF THEY DID KNOW TO TRY TO PROTECT WHOEVER IT IS THEY WANNA PROTECT, BUT I SERIOUSLY DON'T KNOW!!

ARE YOU STUPID?! HOW MANY TIMES DO I HAVE TO TELL YOU?!

I REALLY DON'T KNOW!!

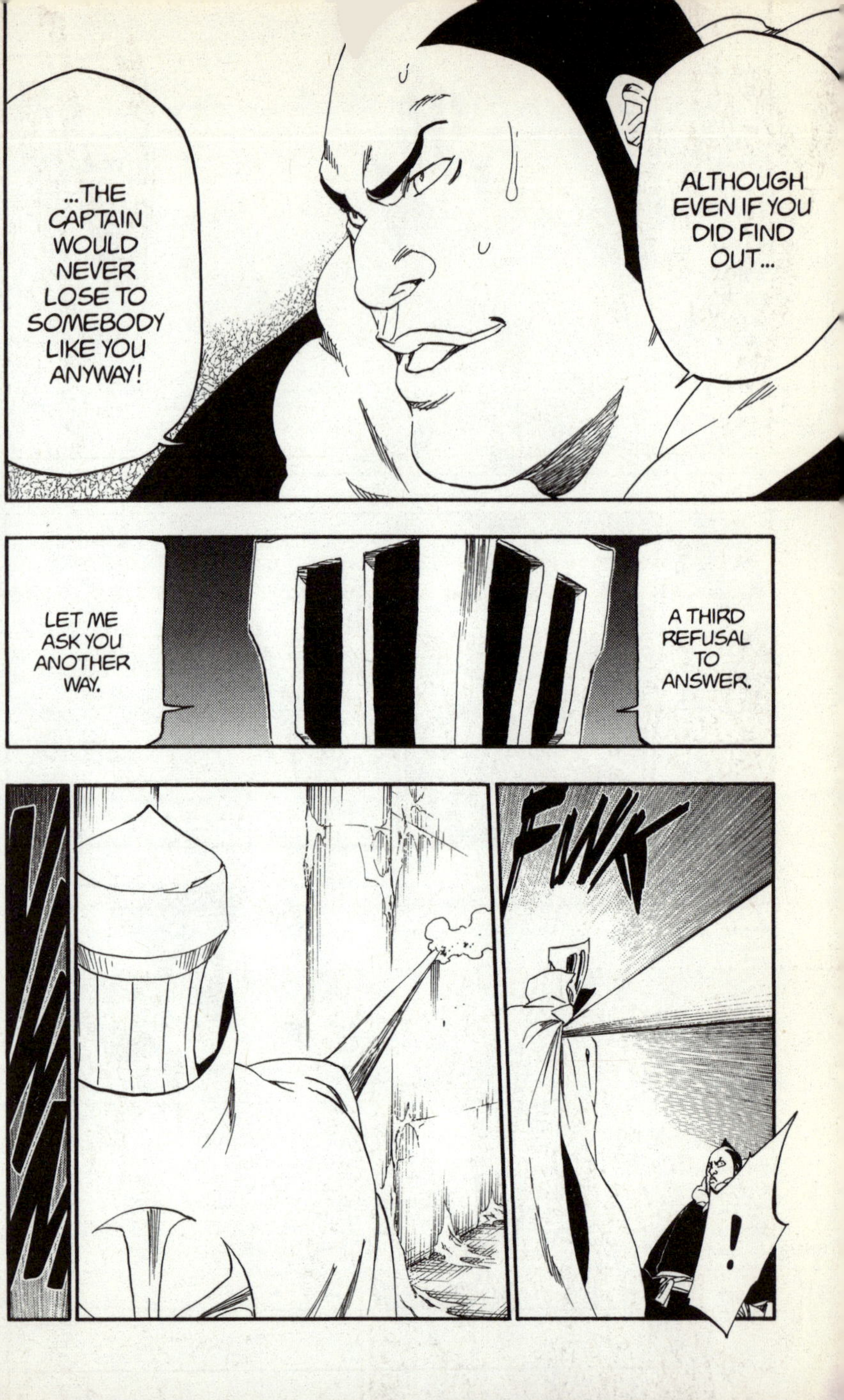
ALTHOUGH EVEN IF YOU DID FIND OUT...
...THE CAPTAIN WOULD NEVER LOSE TO SOMEBODY LIKE YOU ANYWAY!
A THIRD REFUSAL TO ANSWER.
LET ME ASK YOU ANOTHER WAY.
FWK
!

KRUK

WHAT THE HELL ARE YOU...

KOFF?!

BIG...

BROTH-ER...

MARE...

...CHIYO...

SHE'S FAMILY, ISN'T SHE?
YOU DON'T HAVE TO TELL ME.
HER PHYSICAL APPEARANCE MATCH RATIO IS QUITE LOW, BUT THE SPIRITUAL PRESSURE MATCH RATIO TO YOU IS OVER 50%.
ALSO ...
...I DETECT THREE OTHER INDIVIDUALS THAT HAVE A SPIRITUAL PRESSURE MATCH RATIO OF OVER 50%...
...WITHIN A 30-METER RADIUS.
ALL OF THEM...
...WILL DIE THE EXACT MOMENT OF YOUR NEXT REFUSAL TO ANSWER.
GADONK

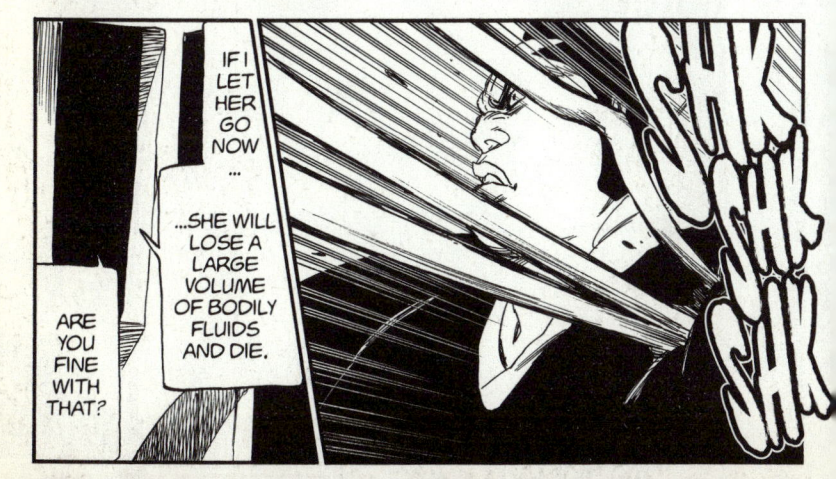

LET MAREYO GO!!

KTNK.

CAN I...
...TAKE THIS AS A REFUSAL TO ANSWER?

I HAVE TWO QUESTIONS...

IF I LET HER GO NOW...

...SHE WILL LOSE A LARGE VOLUME OF BODILY FLUIDS AND DIE.

ARE YOU FINE WITH THAT?

SHK SHK SHK

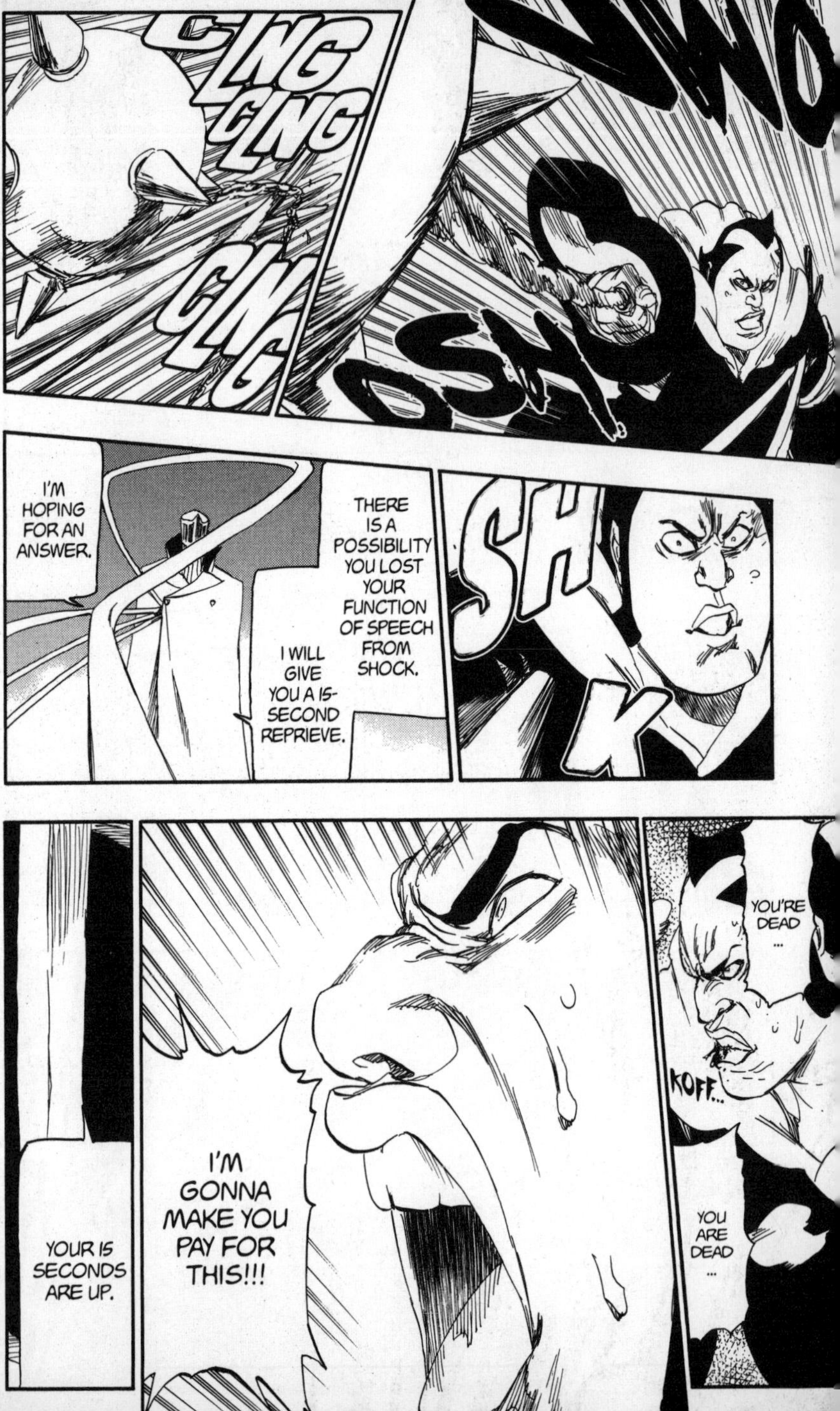
CLNG
CLNG
CLNG
THERE IS A POSSIBILITY YOU LOST YOUR FUNCTION OF SPEECH FROM SHOCK.
I WILL GIVE YOU A 15-SECOND REPRIEVE.
I'M HOPING FOR AN ANSWER.
YOU'RE DEAD ...
KOFF...
YOU ARE DEAD ...
I'M GONNA MAKE YOU PAY FOR THIS!!!
YOUR 15 SECONDS ARE UP.

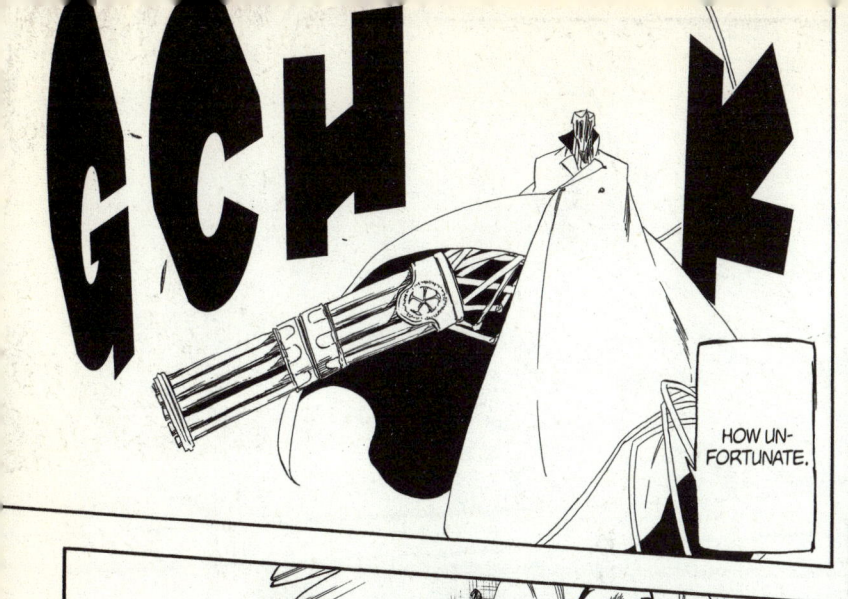

GCHK

How un- fortunate.

You bastaaaard!!!

KAKAK
KAKAK

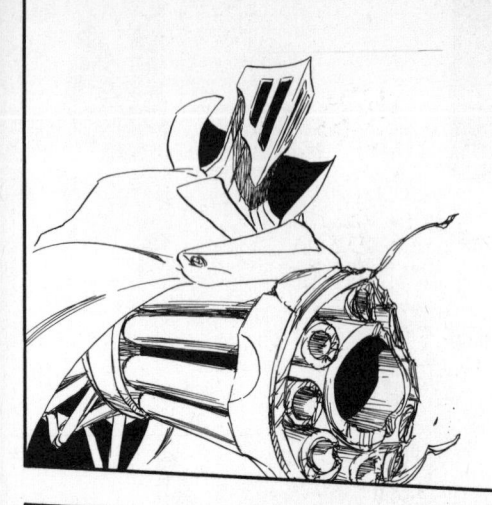

?!

I WOULD'VE EXPECTED A QUINCY TO USE A BOW AND ARROW...

GSHANK

WOOOO

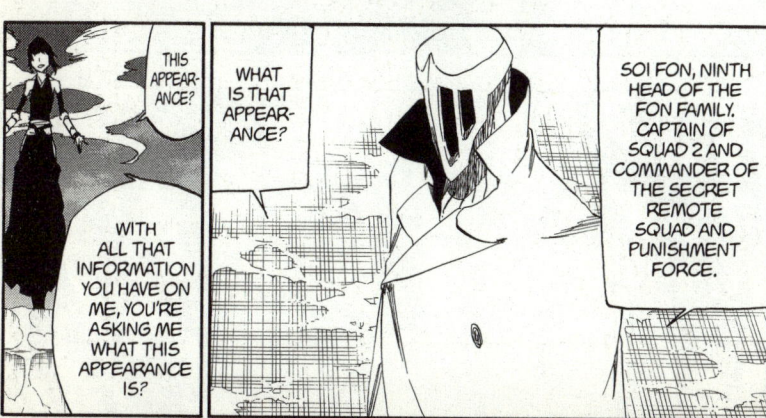

"YOU'RE A LOT MORE SOPHISTICATED THAN I HAD HEARD.

"DID YOU THINK THE SECRET REMOTE SQUAD COULDN'T CLOAK THEIR SPIRITUAL PRESSURE?"

"THERE WAS NO READING ON MY SENSOR..."

"THIS APPEARANCE?"

"WHAT IS THAT APPEARANCE?"

"WITH ALL THAT INFORMATION YOU HAVE ON ME, YOU'RE ASKING ME WHAT THIS APPEARANCE IS?"

SOI FON, NINTH HEAD OF THE FON FAMILY. CAPTAIN OF SQUAD 2 AND COMMANDER OF THE SECRET REMOTE SQUAD AND PUNISHMENT FORCE.

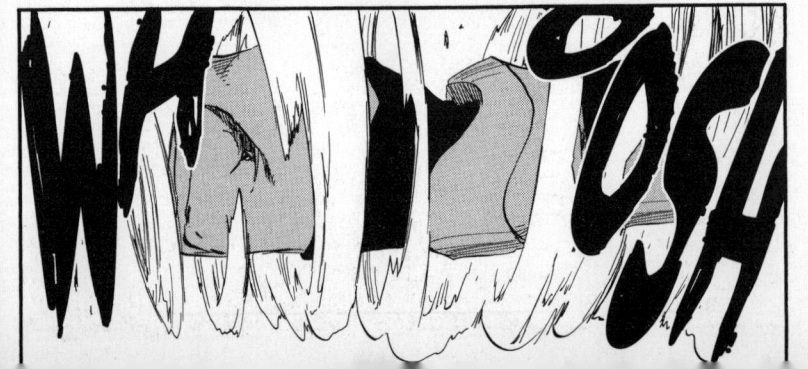

IT'S SHUNKO.

DID YOU THINK I WOULD LET IT STAY UNPERFECTED?

BUT YOUR SHUNKO SHOULD STILL BE UNPERFECTED.

I KNOW. THE HIGHEST FORM OF HAKUDA COMBAT ART OF FIGHTING BY BEARING KIDO ON BOTH YOUR BACK AND SHOULDERS.

AND UNTIL TODAY, I HAVE BEEN TRAINING TO IMPROVE IT EVEN FURTHER.

I PERFECTED SHUNKO AFTER MY BATTLE WITH YORUICHI.

WHOOSH

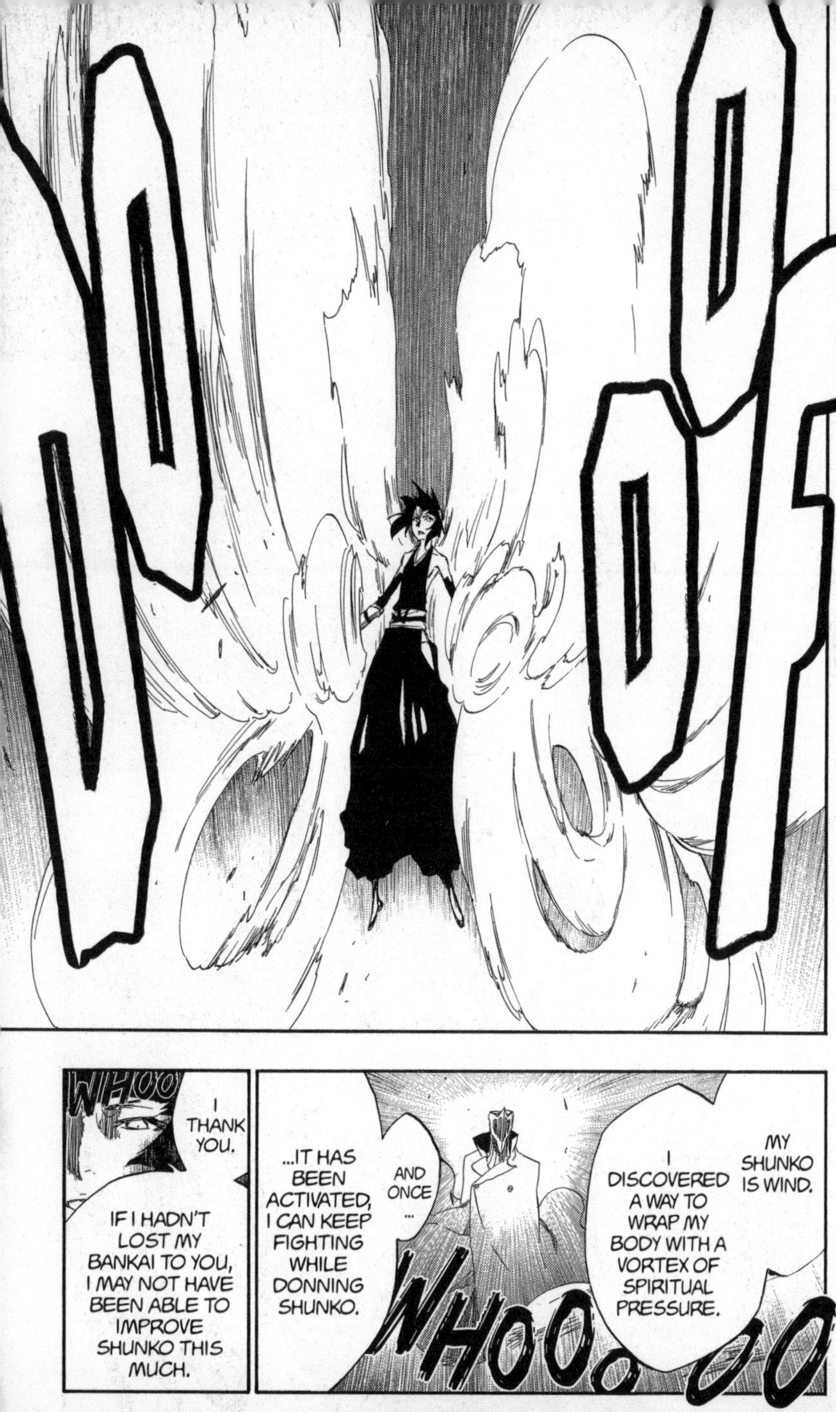
MY SHUNKO IS WIND.
I DISCOVERED A WAY TO WRAP MY BODY WITH A VORTEX OF SPIRITUAL PRESSURE.
AND ONCE...
...IT HAS BEEN ACTIVATED, I CAN KEEP FIGHTING WHILE DONNING SHUNKO.
WHOO...OO
WHOO
I THANK YOU.
IF I HADN'T LOST MY BANKAI TO YOU, I MAY NOT HAVE BEEN ABLE TO IMPROVE SHUNKO THIS MUCH.

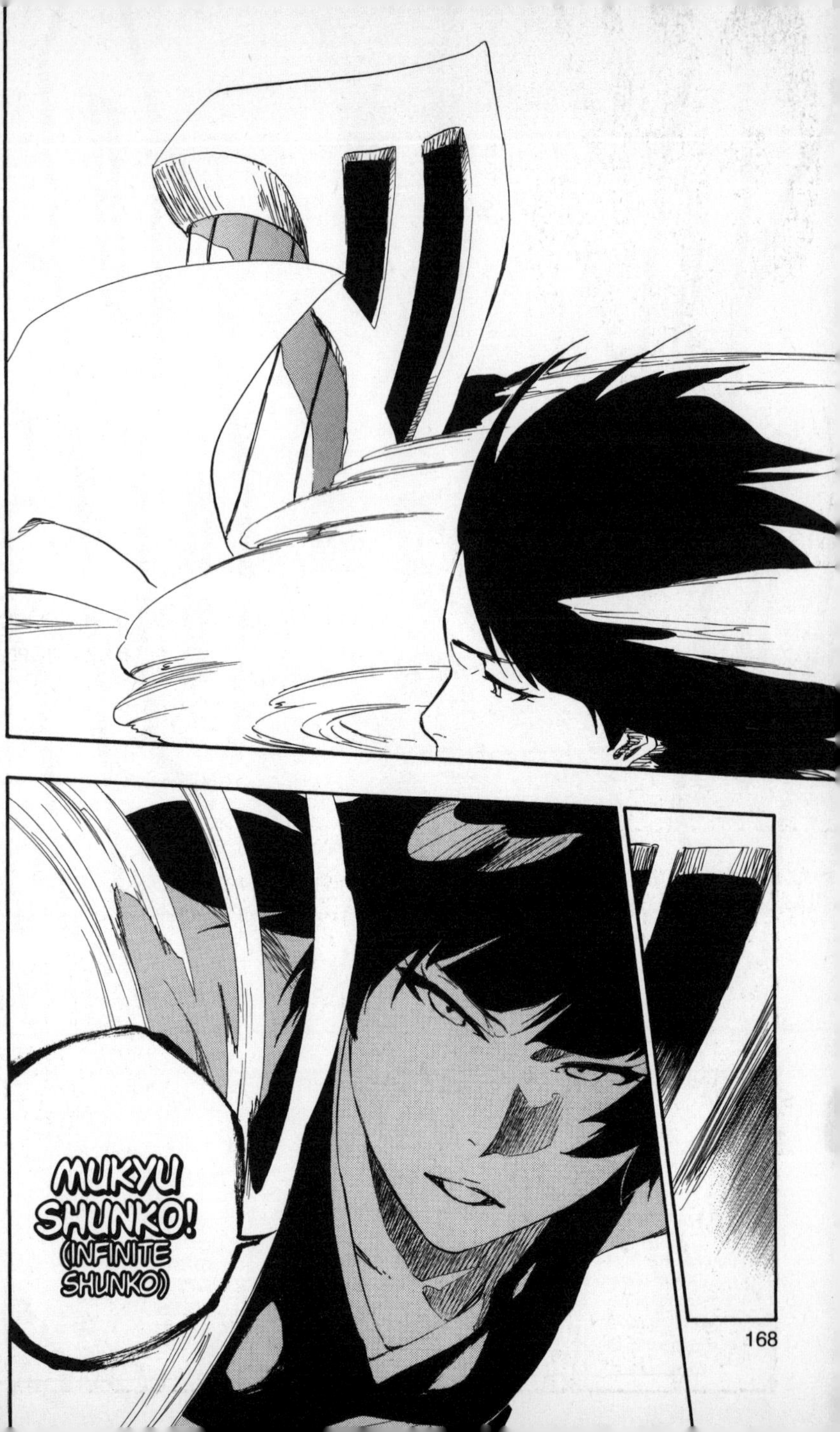
MUKYU SHUNKO!
(INFINITE SHUNKO)

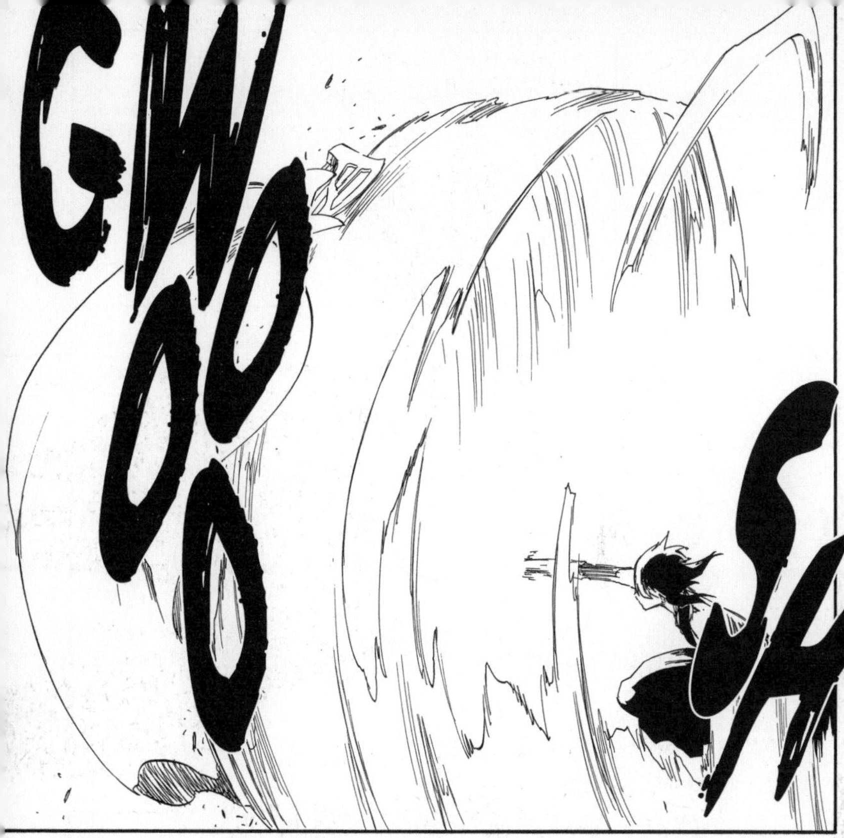
GWOOOO
SH

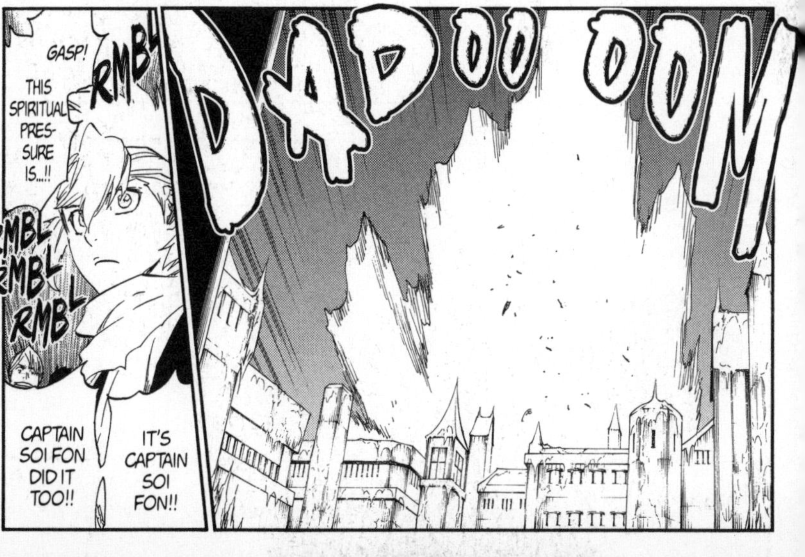
DADOOOOM
RMBL
GASP!
THIS SPIRITUAL PRES-SURE IS...!!
RMBL RMBL RMBL
IT'S CAPTAIN SOI FON!!
CAPTAIN SOI FON DID IT TOO!!

BUT...

MAY-BE...

THINGS ARE LOOKING UP, CAPTAIN.

SHALL WE GO HELP THE OTHER CAPTAINS?

HEY, HEY, HEY...

C'MON, MAN.

YOU GONNA LEAVE ME HANGING HERE WHILE WE'RE STILL WARMING UP?

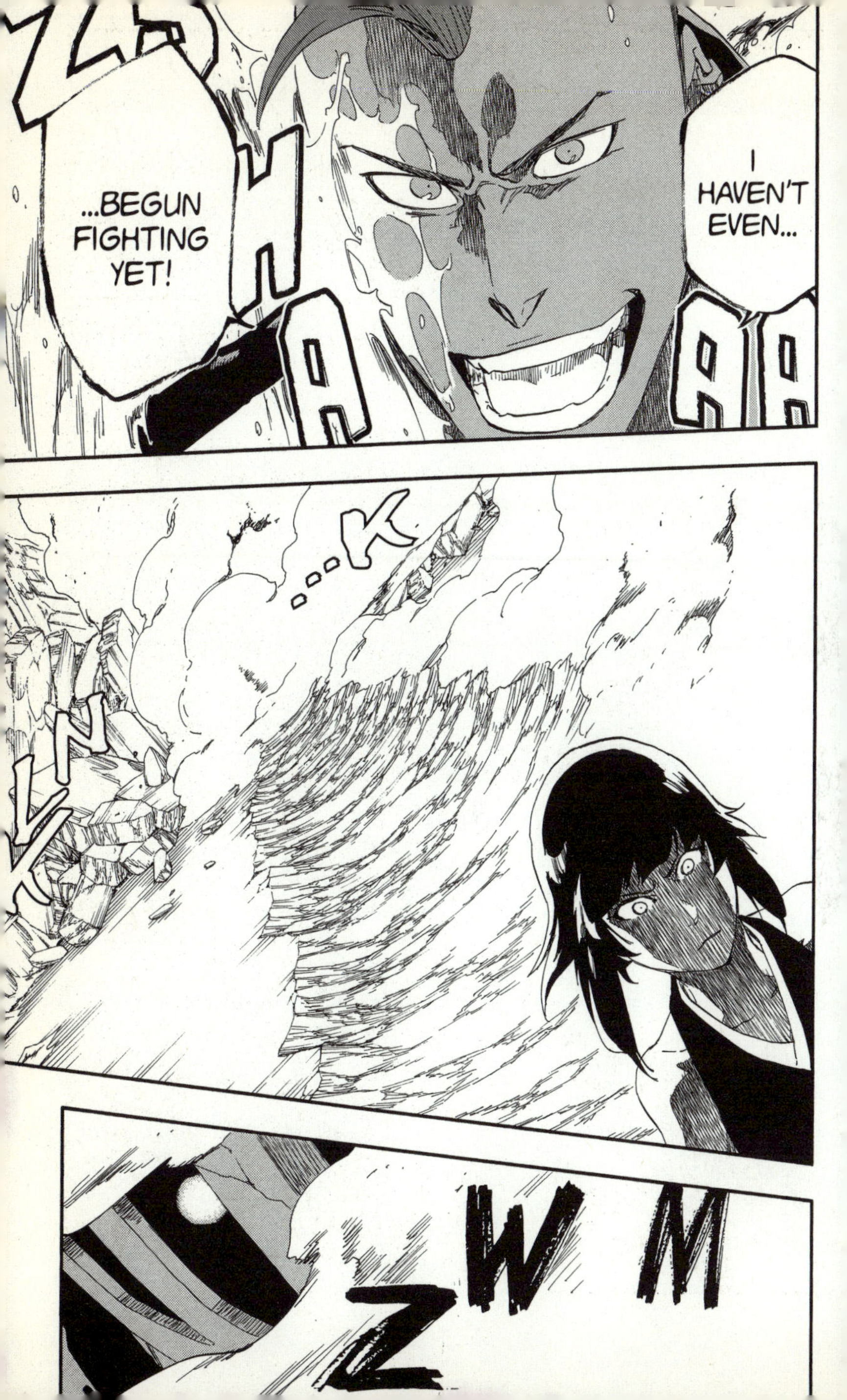
I HAVEN'T EVEN...
...BEGUN FIGHTING YET!
ZWM

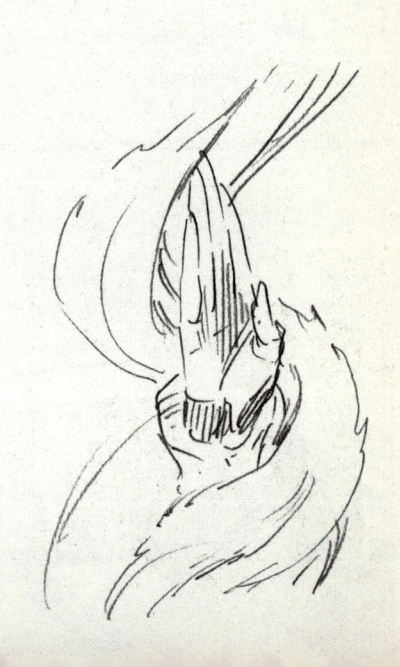

MMM... MM...

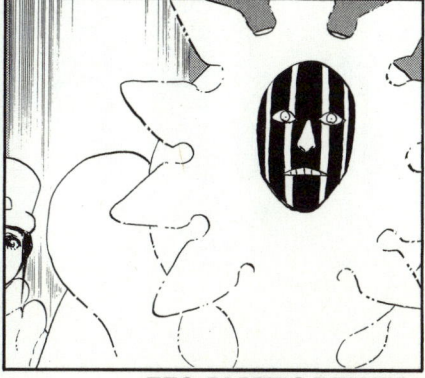

NOT HAPPENING!

I'M GONNA PASS.

I GET THE FEELING YOU'LL TAKE TOO LONG.

550. BLAZING BULLETS

TAKE TOO LONG?
WHAT DO YOU MEAN?
FOR YOU TO DIE.
WAY TOO MANY SCENARIOS TO TEST OUT.
I...
...REALLY HATE THOSE KINDS OF LITTLE THINGS.
I LIKE TO ZIP RIGHT THROUGH IT.
YOU SHOULD GO FIND SOMEBODY ELSE TO FIGHT.
GOOD-BYE.
TMP
TMP
TMP
TMP...
AREN'T YOU GOING TO STOP ME...?
NO.
GO WHEREVER YOU PLEASE.

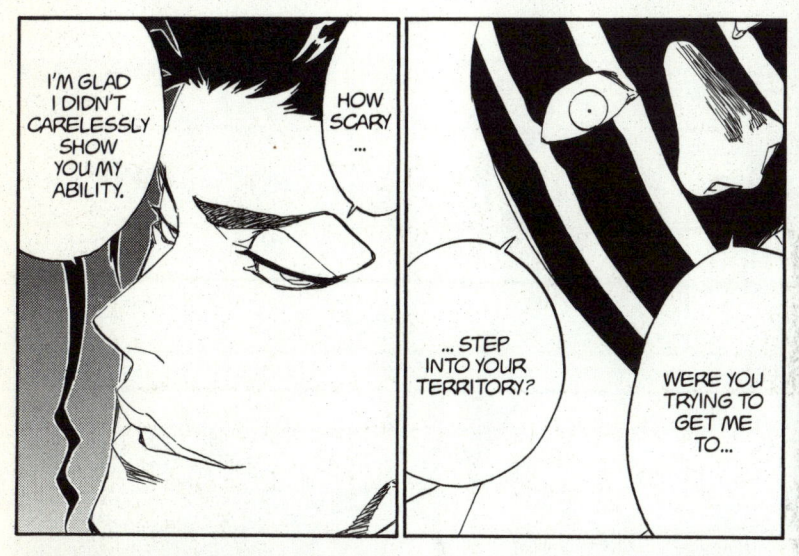

OR WHAT?

I WOULD LIKE SOME TIME MYSELF TO ANALYZE YOUR SPIRITUAL PRESSURE.

HOW SCARY...

I'M GLAD I DIDN'T CARELESSLY SHOW YOU MY ABILITY.

WERE YOU TRYING TO GET ME TO...

...STEP INTO YOUR TERRITORY?

ZOM...!M

I KNEW IT...

IT SEEMS SO!

IT SEEMS SHE DEFEATED THE ENEMY WITHOUT HAVING BANKAI!

RMBL RMBL

SOI FON, THIS SPIRITUAL PRESSURE IS...

JUST AS HIS MAJESTY PREDICTED.

...WILL LEARN HOW TO FIGHT WITHOUT IT IN A SHORT PERIOD OF TIME.

THE CAPTAINS WHO LOST THEIR BANKAI...

IF IT WAS PREDICTED...

I KNOW YOU... ...KNOW WHAT THAT MEANS.

...IT MEANS THE SITUATION...

...IS STILL CRITICAL FOR YOUR SIDE.

BLEACH 550.

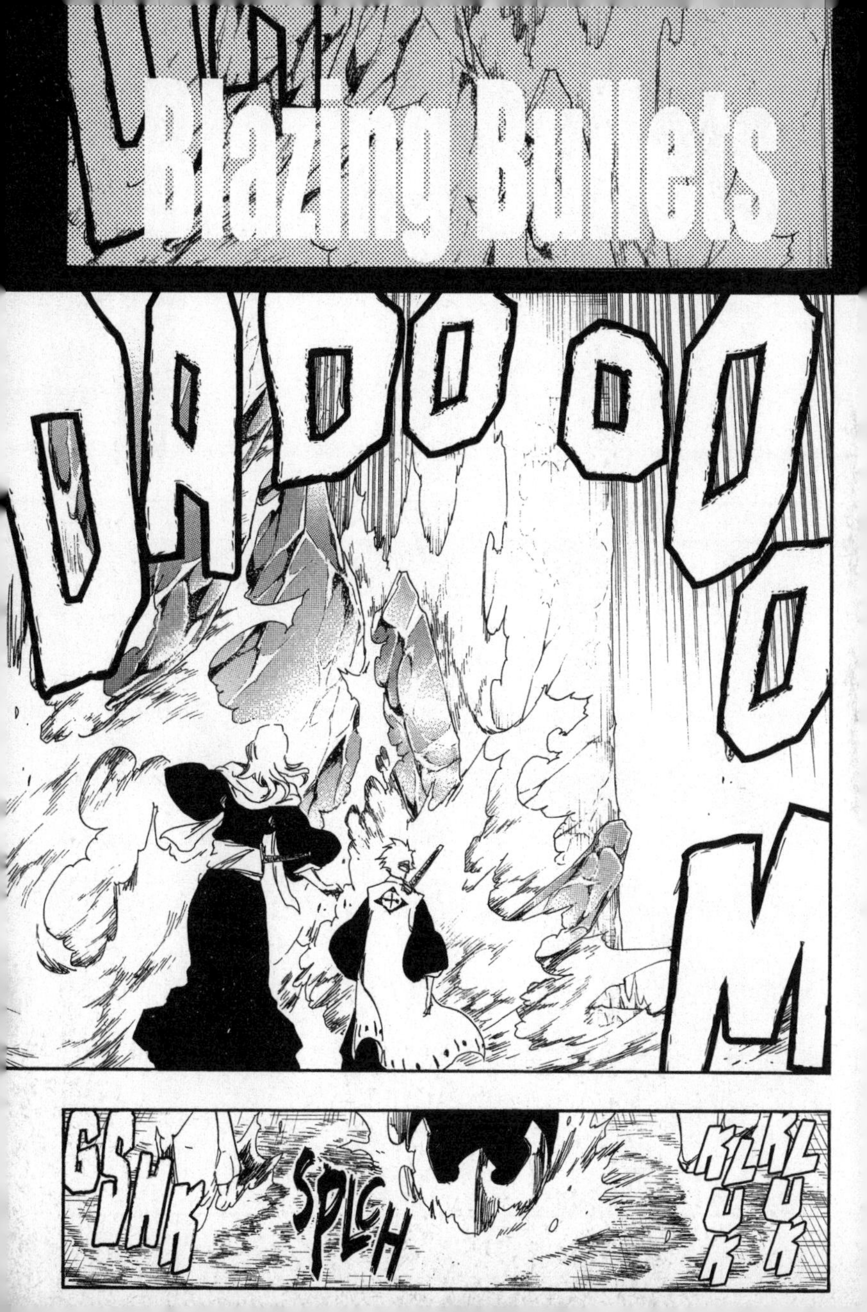
Blazing Bullets
GSHK
SPLCH
KLUK
KLUK

HE SHOULDA BEEN RIPPED APART BY CAPTAIN HITSUGAYA'S ICE...

N... HE... NO WAY...

LOOK. MY BEST STERN RITTER UNIFORM IS RUINED.

AT LEAST MY CAPE WAS.

I *WAS* RIPPED APART.

GCHK

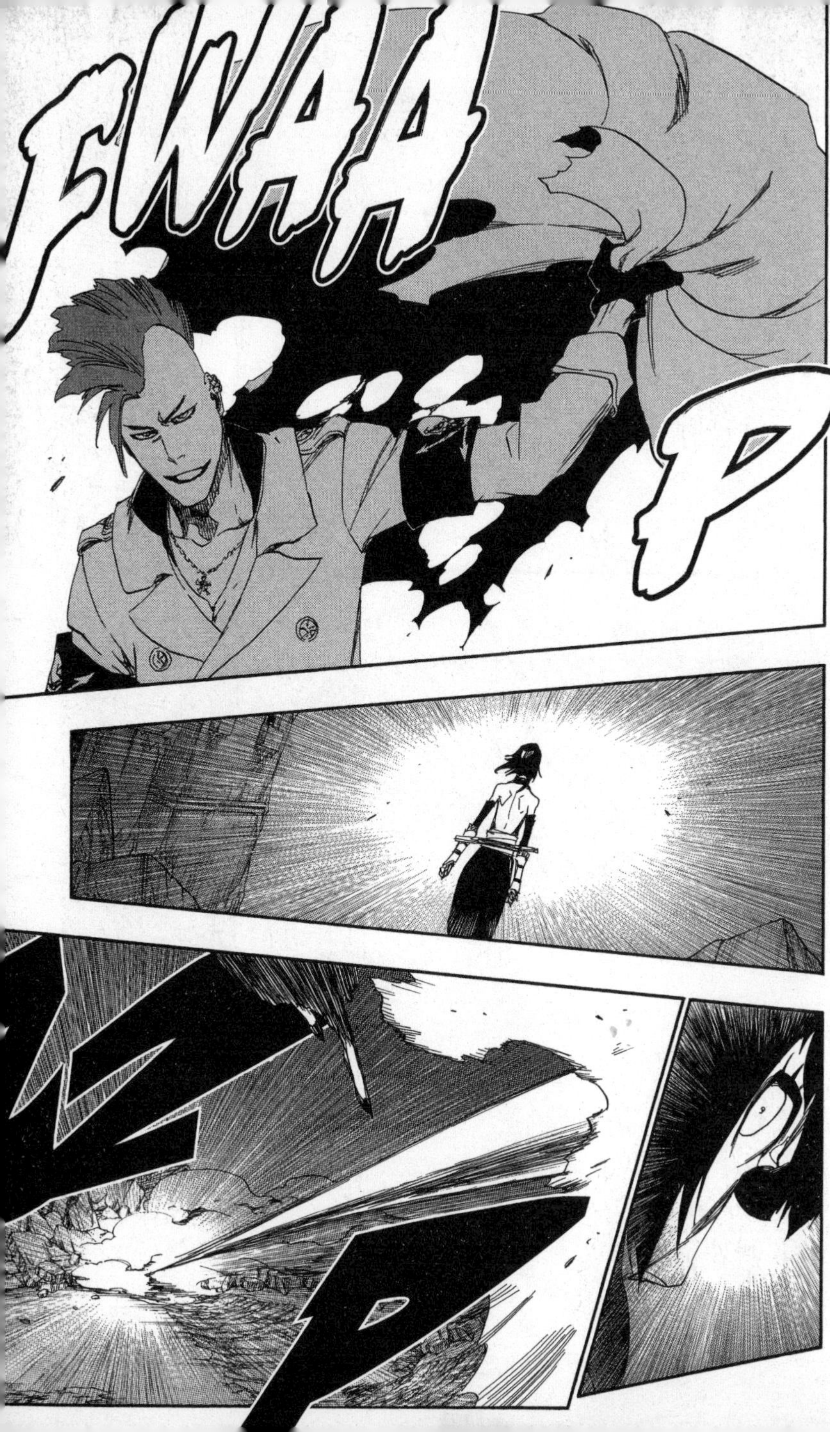
FWAAP

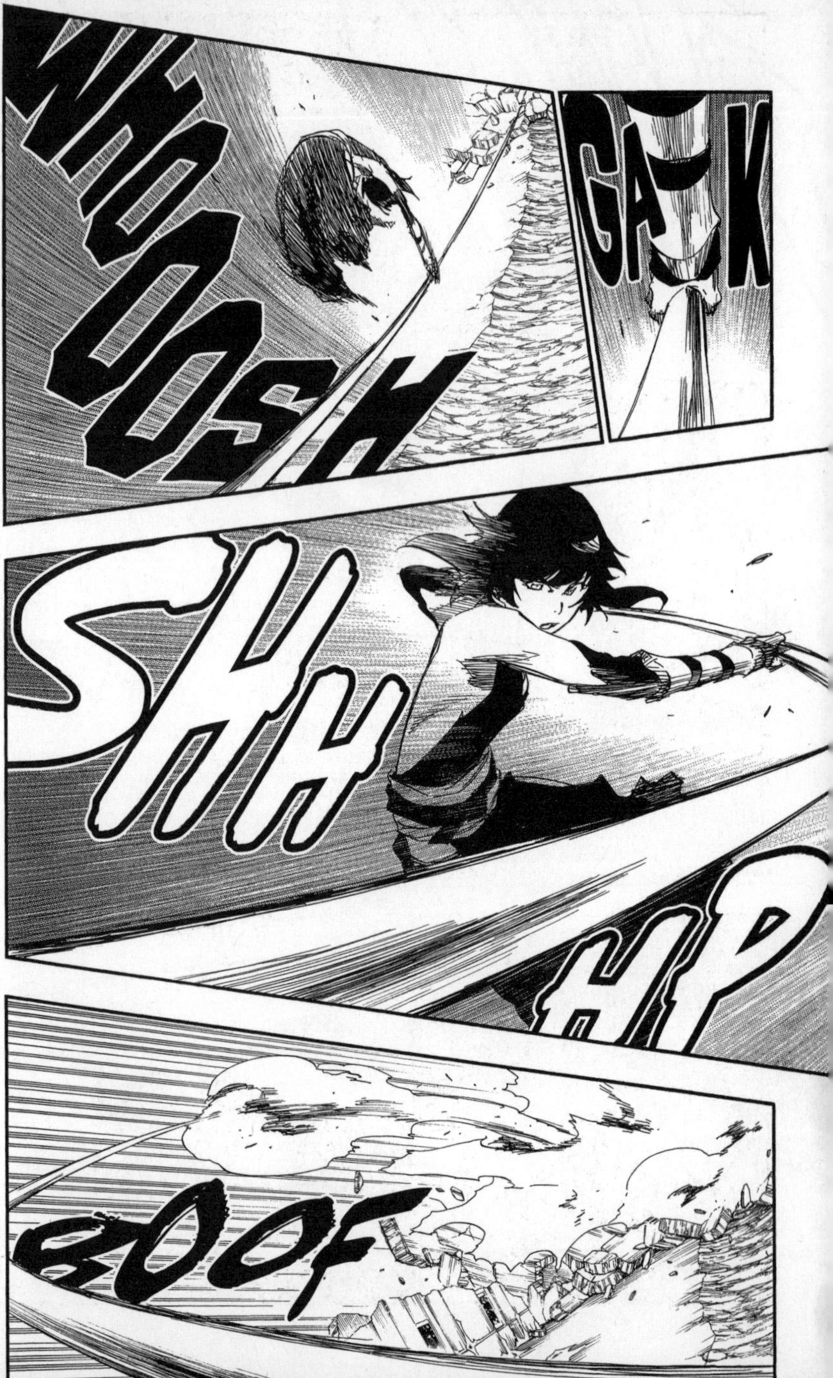
GAK
WHOOSH
SHH
HP
BOOF

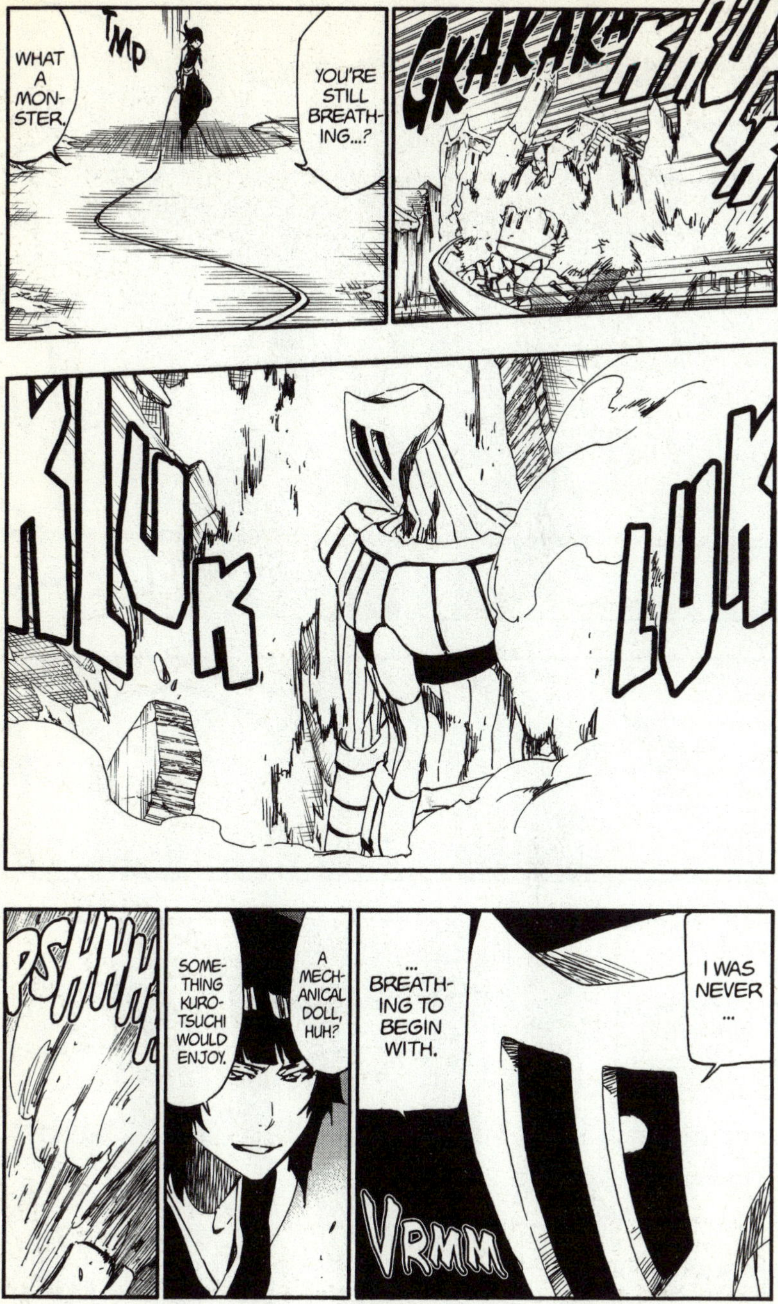
GKAKAKA
YOU'RE STILL BREATHING...?
TMP
WHAT A MONSTER.
KLUK
LUK
I WAS NEVER ...
... BREATHING TO BEGIN WITH.
VRMM
A MECHANICAL DOLL, HUH?
SOMETHING KUROTSUCHI WOULD ENJOY.
PSHHH

SCHK

MUKYU SHUNKO.

I HAVE RECEIVED VERY USEFUL DATA. HOW- EVER...

...AT THE SAME TIME, I AM DISAPPOINTED.

AT YOUR CURRENT LEVEL, THERE IS NO NEED TO USE THE BANKAI I TOOK FROM YOU.

BZMMMMMM

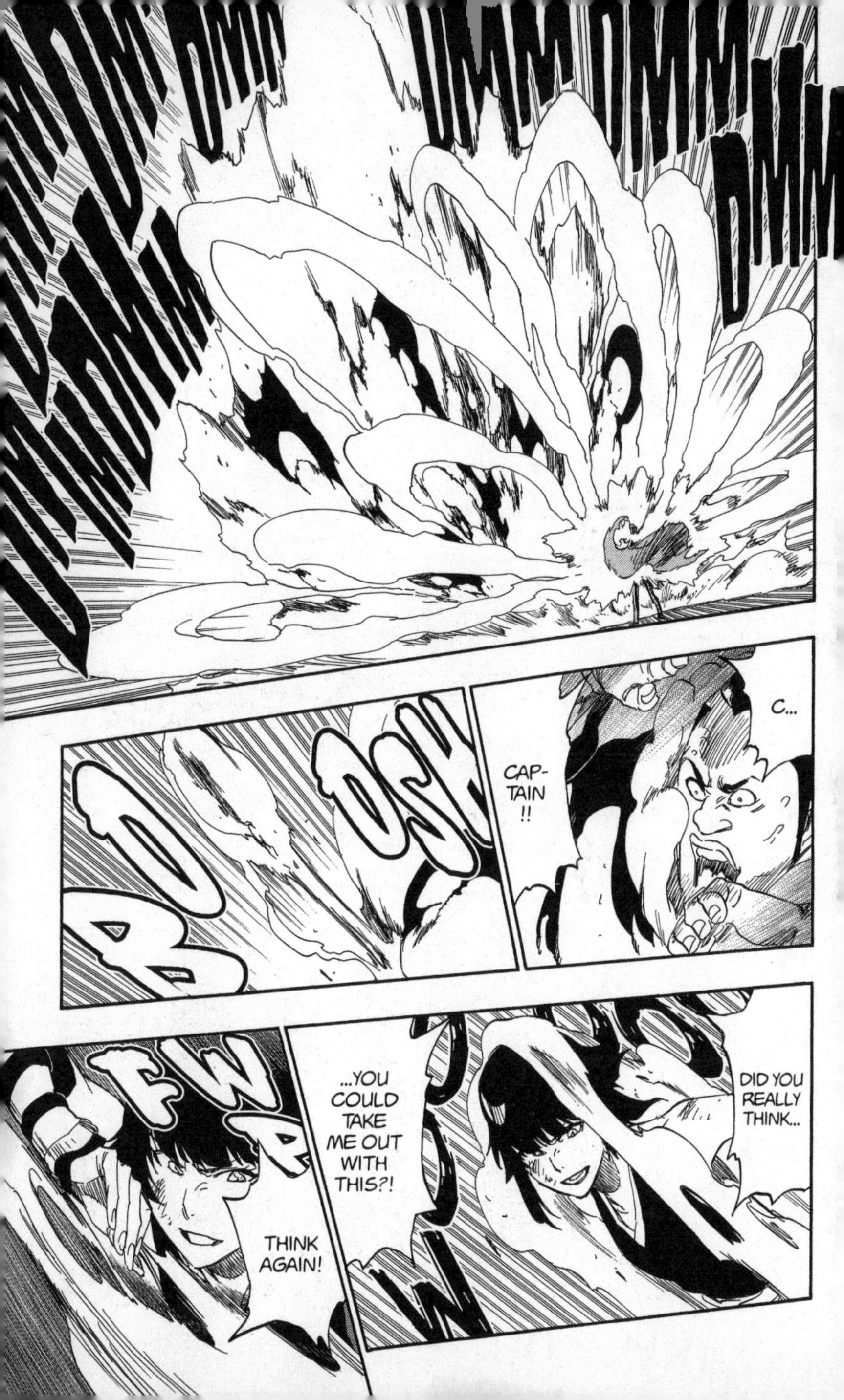
C...
CAP-TAIN!!
DID YOU REALLY THINK...
...YOU COULD TAKE ME OUT WITH THIS?!
THINK AGAIN!

!!!
I TOLD YOU.
I HAVE RECEIVED...
...USEFUL DATA ON MUKYU SHUNKO.
DAMN IT...
BZMM...M

LET ME TELL YOU SOMETHING. YOU SAID YOU COULD SHIELD MY FLAME EARLIER.

SO WHY DO YOU THINK WE'RE STILL ALIVE? HE DIDN'T MISS. WE WERE ALL DIRECTLY STRUCK BY IT.

THE STERN RITTERS WHO WERE BURNED BY YOUR CAPTAIN GENERAL... ...ARE ALL ALIVE. INCLUDING ME.

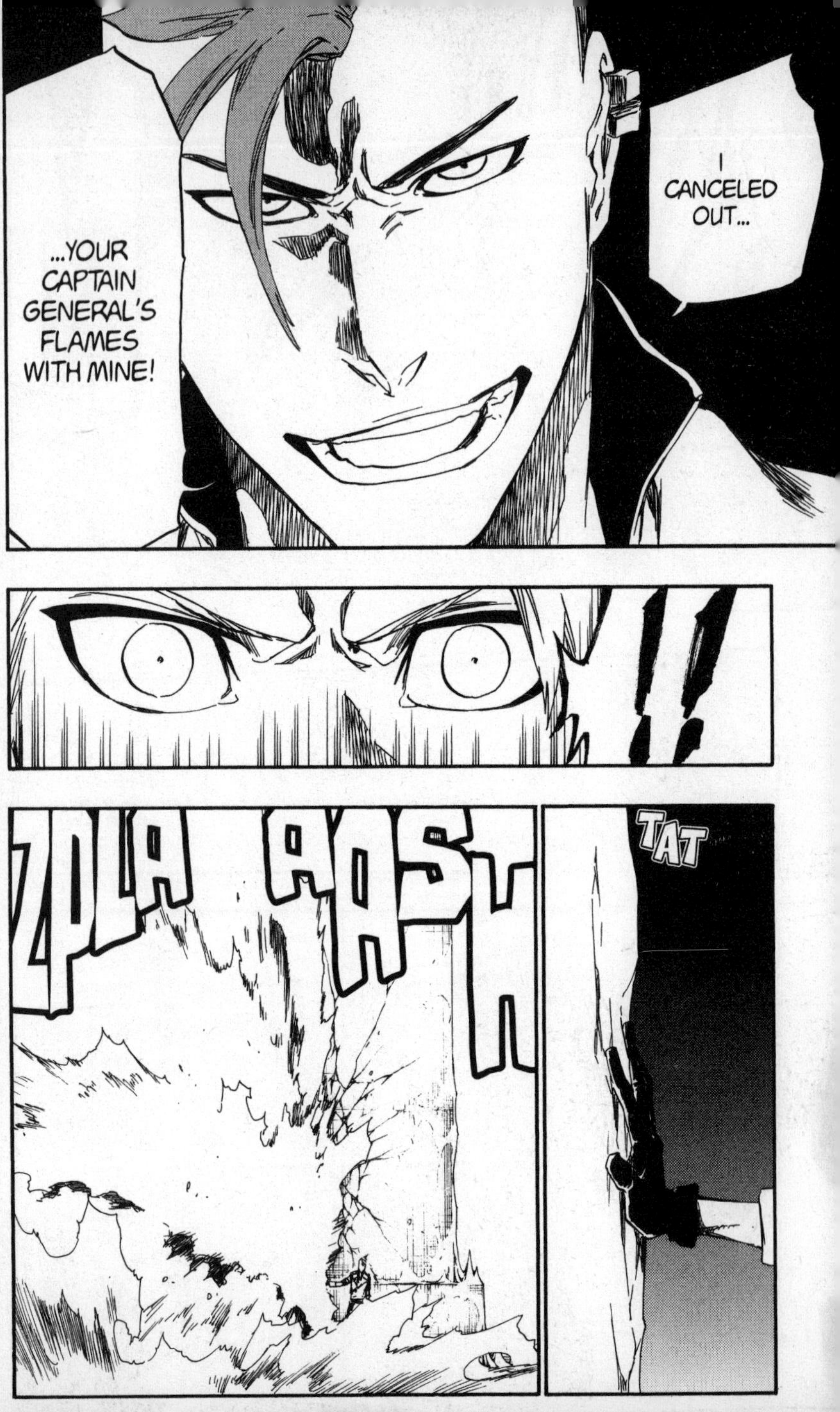
I CANCELED OUT...
...YOUR CAPTAIN GENERAL'S FLAMES WITH MINE!
TAT
ZPLA AASH

IT'S TOO BAD YOU DON'T HAVE BANKAI RIGHT NOW.
I COULD'VE SHOWN YOU...
...THAT I ONLY NEED A FINGER TO FIGHT AGAINST YOUR ICE.
GWOOF
SPLAASH!

IT WON'T REACH ME.

YES, SIR!

MATSUMOTO, FALL BACK! WE NEED TO REGROUP!!

I'LL DELAY HIM WITH MY RYOJIN HYOHEKI ICE WALL!

BUT I'LL TELL YOU THIS.

A WALL OF FINELY WOVEN ICE.

ZSHAAA

YOU CAN TRY WHATEVER YOU WANT WITH YOUR ICE...

YOU GOT A LOT UP YOUR SLEEVES.

...BUT ALL I NEED IS A FINGER.

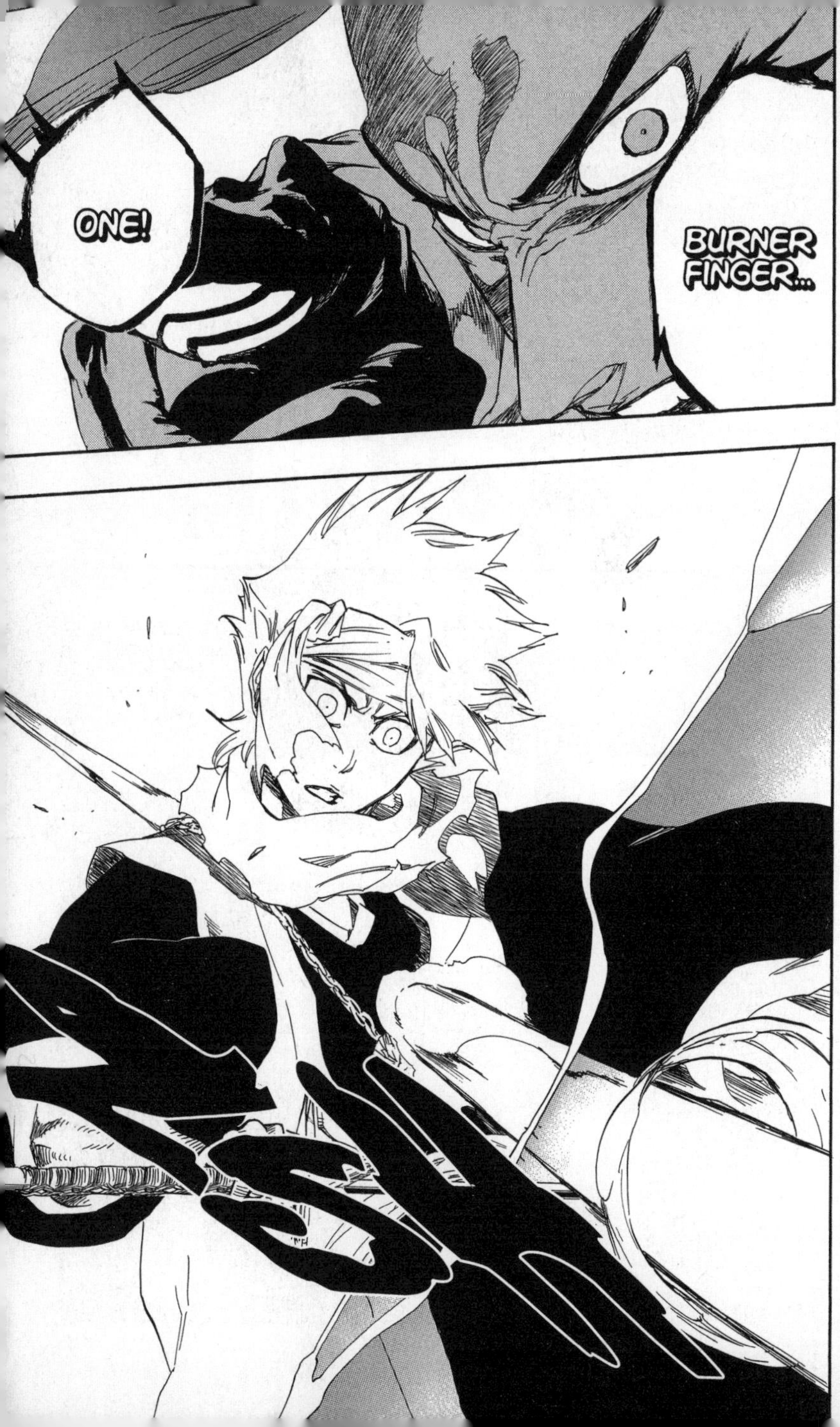
BURNER FINGER...
ONE!

CONTINUED IN BLEACH 62

DISCOVER ANIME
IN A WHOLE NEW WAY!

www.neonalley.com

What it is...

- Streaming anime delivered 24/7 straight to your TV via your connected video game console
- All English dubbed content
- Anime, martial arts movies, and more

Go to **neonalley.com** for news, updates and to see if Neon Alley is available in your area.

NEON ALLEY is a trademark or service mark of VIZ Media, LLC.

You're Reading in the Wrong Direction!!

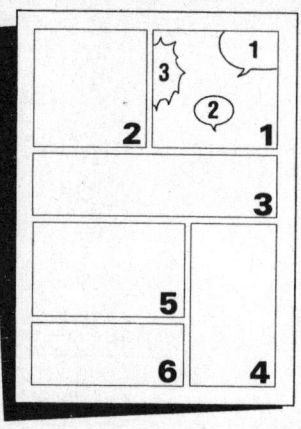

Whoops! Guess what? You're starting at the wrong end of the comic!

...It's true! In keeping with the original Japanese format, **Bleach** is meant to be read from right to left, starting in the upper-right corner.

Unlike English, which is read from left to right, Japanese is read from right to left, meaning that action, sound effects and word-balloon order are completely reversed... something which can make readers unfamiliar with Japanese feel pretty backwards themselves. For this reason, manga or Japanese comics published in the U.S. in English have sometimes been published "flopped"—that is, printed in exact reverse order, as though seen from the other side of a mirror.

By flopping pages, U.S. publishers can avoid confusing readers, but the compromise is not without its downside. For one thing, a character in a flopped manga series who once wore in the original Japanese version a T-shirt emblazoned with "M A Y" (as in "the merry month of") now wears one which reads "Y A M"! Additionally, many manga creators in Japan are themselves unhappy with the process, as some feel the mirror-imaging of their art skews their original intentions.

We are proud to bring you Tite Kubo's **Bleach** in the original unflopped format. For now, though, turn to the other side of the book and let the adventure begin...!

—Editor